Song of Joy

Song of Joy

A Little Girl in the Hands of a Big God

Joanie Shawhan

GRACELEAF
PUBLISHING

Song of Joy: A Little Girl in the Hands of a Big God
Copyright © 2025 Joanie Shawhan
www.joanieshawhan.com
Published by Graceleaf Publishing
ISBN: 979-8-9997127-0-7

For privacy reasons, names have been changed. This book is inspired by the life of Anna Joy (a pseudonym) and written to the best of my recollection of events and memories she shared with me.

Editing, interior design, and cover design by Michelle Rayburn missionandmedia.com

Cover image from DepositPhotos, Ikostudios (photo id 194515954)

2025 First Edition

In loving memory of this woman of faith whose life and love continue to inspire us. And to all our spiritual mothers and fathers—thank you for your unwavering encouragement, your prayers, and for believing in us when we needed it most.

Contents

Foreword

I met the heroine of this memoir, a beloved friend and saint, when I was a new believer in Jesus (Messiah Yeshua). Her example accelerated my spiritual growth, and her prophetic voice confirmed my calling (especially when I was dragging my feet).

My life story includes supernatural visions of the Lord, callings that dramatically redirected my life, and trials through which God tested my faith. Yet when I consider this woman of God, let alone other saints like her in Hebrews 11, how feeble are my steps of faith! Her life story encouraged my faith and obedience to the Holy Spirit, as it did for many others who appear in this book. Even after we moved away so I could pursue a career, my wife and I remained close to our "spiritual mama," visiting her twice a year, and inviting her (and the author) to visit us.

Joanie Shawhan has masterfully taken the raw material of a lived experience and crafted it into a narrative that is both deeply personal and universally relatable. This book beautifully captures the essence of a life of extraordinary challenges and faith-filled triumphs, harsh pain, and ecstatic joy. Few others have lived such a life—the closest I can think of is Teresa of Avila, who also saw herself (together with all who trust and obey the Lord) as the bride of the most glorious Bridegroom. Our heroine experienced many extraordinary visions of the Lord and His powerful angels yet remained meek like her Master. Despite her suffering, she relished joys on earth as well as in heaven.

The Spirit of God guides all who trust in Him through each of our unique challenges, triumphs, tribulations, and joy—which is our strength. I have no doubt that you who read on will be strengthened in your own walk through the valley of shifting shadows, wondering at times where God is, and then discovering that He is your Shepherd, faithfully guiding you until you dine at His wedding table and dwell in the House of the Lord, *l'olam va-ed*, forever and ever.

Dr. Glenn David Blank is now Messianic Rabbi of Beit Simcha (House of Joy) congregation in Allentown, Pennsylvania, Literary Editor for the *Tree of Life Version* (TLV) of the Bible, member of the Tikkun America Apostolic Team, husband, father, and "pop-pop." His testimony is available on YouTube.

A Note from the Author

" Jesus loves you, and I love you too."
I spun around, searching for the person who spoke these words. Then I spotted her—hunched over her crutches and smiling at me. *She doesn't even know me.*

So began my friendship with the woman whom many others and I called our spiritual mother. Every once in a while, God brings people across our path who impact us for the rest of our lives. Anna Joy was one of those people. She prayed with me and for me, taught me the Scriptures, spoke God's wisdom into my life, and emulated the love of Jesus. Anna Joy loved Jesus with all her heart. He was her great delight and her best friend.

An Easterseals poster child with cerebral palsy may seem an unlikely hero of faith. She was devoted to Jesus, which often resulted in being misunderstood. She was a prayer warrior, an intercessor. Her love for her Savior could not be quenched despite suffering loss, betrayal, and disabilities associated with cerebral palsy.

Anna Joy loved people. She placed others' needs above her own, day and night, whether she was sick or in pain. I know few people who have walked at the level of holiness and faithfulness to Jesus that Anna Joy did, amid great suffering. At the same time, the Lord manifested his presence to her and through her in ways few may have seen in modern times.

Anna Joy shared her story with me over the years. Each chapter portrays a snapshot from her life—her struggles, her joys, and her triumphs. Her stories are filled with life lessons, wisdom, God's provision, and his glory. I changed Anna Joy's name as well as the names of each person mentioned in the book to protect their identities. At times I needed to fill in descriptions and dialogue for the settings of her story, but I stayed true to the details she shared with me.

Maybe you are wondering where God's presence has been during your pain. Is it possible God has a greater purpose in suffering? A more glorious plan?

The more Anna Joy suffered, the closer she drew to Jesus. May you be inspired and encouraged as you glimpse portraits of a life lived to the glory of God.

Joanie

1.

Something Is Wrong

For you formed my inward parts; you knitted
me together in my mother's womb. I praise you,
for I am fearfully and wonderfully made.

Psalm 139:13-14 (ESV)

"You do not have the flu or some other intestinal disorder." The doctor's face couldn't conceal his astonishment, and he smiled at Betty. "You are pregnant. I'd say you are due in another three and a half months."

Betty's initial shock gave way to a hint of excitement. Now to tell Earl when he came home from his music gig.

"You know, I haven't been feeling good lately," she said to Earl. "I went to the doctor today, and you'll never guess what he said." She paused. "I'm pregnant."

"Pregnant!" He roared as he balled his hand into a fist.

Betty drew back, hunched over, and clasped her arms around her baby.

Earl thrust his fist, hurtling his rejection toward his unborn child. "I don't want to be saddled with a kid." He swore as he stalked away, slugging his beer. "It better be a boy."

.ఆపఌ.

Several weeks later, labor pains pulsated throughout Betty's abdomen and into her back. The hospital staff rushed her into the delivery room, flung her legs into the stirrups the second she was on the birthing table, and shoved the gas mask over her mouth. *How could this be happening? I still have three months to go.*

After only a few pushes, the nurse cradled the six-month preemie, a baby girl, in the palm of her hand. Shaking her head, she laid the baby in an incubator infused with 100 percent oxygen. "I'll call the priest," she said. Two-pound infants rarely survived.

"What's the baby's name?" the priest asked when he entered the room.

"Anna Joy," the mother replied.

The priest sprinkled holy water on the baby's head and anointed her with oil. "I baptize you, Anna Joy, in the name of the Father, the Son, and the Holy Spirit."

.ₒₒℓₑₒ.

Betty looked up as a nurse clad in starched whites entered the waiting room with a clipboard in her hand. "Anna Joy?" She tucked an unruly curl back under her starched nursing cap.

Betty pulled her daughter to her chest, the child's ringlets brushing her red-rouged cheek. They followed the nurse into the exam room.

Momentarily, the doctor walked into the room and sat down across from Betty. "Good morning. What brings you here today?"

"My daughter's a year old and doesn't sit up or even roll over."

"Well, let's examine her," he said.

Betty laid her daughter on the exam table and removed her dress and diaper. Anna Joy giggled. Instinctively, Betty rested her hand across Anna Joy's tummy to prevent her from rolling off the table. But her baby had never rolled over yet. The mother searched once again for some sign of movement in her legs, even a little kick. But her baby's legs just stiffened, almost scissor-like.

The doctor examined Anna Joy. "Just give her some time. It takes a little longer for premature babies to reach these milestones." He patted her hand. "Don't worry. She'll be fine."

Of course, the doctor is right, Betty thought. *Anna Joy is just a little slower because she was three months premature.*

Each time Betty bathed her baby or changed a diaper, she waited in anticipation. Would today be the day she'd see a flicker of a kick? A rollover attempt? With each passing month, anxiety and worry mounted, crushing her facade of bravery and eroding her hope. *Something's wrong. She's not fine! Do they know and just don't want to tell me?*

·ॐ·

Betty hefted her two-year-old daughter onto her hip and marched into the doctor's office. The clicking of her heels echoed down the corridor. "She's not sitting up by herself, crawling, or walking. Whenever she gets a fever, she has seizures. Something's wrong with my little girl."

Betty propped her daughter up on the exam table. As she stretched her arms toward her mother, Anna Joy bobbled, her blonde curls brushing her crossed eyes.

The doctor picked up a tiny reflex hammer and tapped Anna Joy's elbows and knees. He flipped her over, poked, and prodded. Anna Joy fussed as he checked her muscle tone, coordination, and reflexes. After completing his exam, the doctor handed Anna Joy back to her mother.

"I don't know for sure." He crossed his arms. "But I think your daughter may have cerebral palsy."

"Cerebral palsy? What's that?" She jostled Anna Joy on her knee.

"Cerebral palsy affects muscle movement, coordination, and balance as well as fine motor skills in the hands and fingers. It can also affect speech. There are no specific tests for cerebral palsy." He paused. "And there is no cure."

"Will she walk?" Betty choked on the words.

The doctor pursed his lips, dropping his gaze. When he looked up, he met Betty's eyes and said, "Her muscles are tight and spastic. Therefore, we need to stretch them before she can walk. We can start therapy and teach you to do exercises with her at home. Eventually, we can fit her with leg braces and crutches."

Betty tightened her grip on her daughter to stop the trembling in her hands. "When will she walk?"

"I don't know," he said. "She will need to be evaluated by specialists and have therapy."

Betty sat stunned. *Braces? Crutches?* As she rose from the chair, she teetered on her high heels, grasping the arm for support. She shifted Anna Joy onto her hip, smoothed her Sunday suit, and walked toward the door. "Thank you, doctor." She swiped away a tear.

During the cab ride home, Betty stroked the curls of her sleeping daughter as she lay splayed across her lap. A familiar nausea disrupted her already contorted thoughts. *How am I going to manage a new baby and a crippled child? I can't even find a babysitter!* Betty had no family nearby, and none of her neighbors were willing to stay with a child who spiked fevers and had seizures.

Without a babysitter, Betty could no longer go to her husband's gigs and parties, which lasted well into the night. The demands of staying home with a disabled child had placed an additional strain on their marriage.

2.

Daddy

*"I will be a Father to you, and you will be my sons
and daughters, says the Lord Almighty."*

2 Corinthians 6:18 (NIV)

Anna Joy peeked around the corner. The beat of country-western music reverberated in her heart, beckoning her into the room. There he was—her daddy—strumming his guitar and jamming with country music legends in plaid shirts and cowboy hats. She beamed with pride. A chorus of harmonies permeated the room, mingling with cigarette smoke.

Shhh. She placed her finger on her lips. She had to be careful. If Mommy or Daddy spotted her, she would get spanked and sent to her room. Then she couldn't hear Daddy's music. But Mommy was in the kitchen getting another round of beer for the guests. If Anna Joy could just get to that one corner, she could pull herself up and stand like a big girl. Besides, no one would see her there, enclosed on three sides. She crawled out. Not really a crawl, because her legs moved as one unit.

With each scoot, she pulled the hem of her dress out from under her knees. She glanced around the room and grinned. She'd made it! No one had seen her. She pulled herself up, balancing in her special corner. Immersed in the rhythm of the music, Anna Joy clapped her little hands in glee.

.ⲟꙅℯ᎐.

Anna Joy's mom bustled around the house, preparing for another one of her daddy's parties. Most of the time, his parties were fun, especially when she didn't get spanked and sent to her room. But sometimes the men drank too much and snatched the ladies, pulling them onto their laps despite squeals of protest.

Anna Joy begged her mother to wear the fancy dress. Mom finally acquiesced, but she pointed her finger at Anna Joy. "You stay out of the way of your daddy and his friends."

While Mom was busy taking care of her baby brother, maybe Anna Joy could sneak into the living room and show Daddy her new dress. She peered into the room as a woman sidled up to her daddy and smiled. Daddy smiled back. Anna Joy wished her daddy would smile at her. Maybe he would tell her how pretty she looked in her new ruffled dress.

She scooted around the perimeter of the room to the side of Daddy's chair. Anna Joy grasped the arm of the chair and pulled herself up. "Hi, Daddy."

Daddy frowned. "You're not supposed to be in here. Where's your mother?"

"She's taking care of the baby." Anna Joy grinned. "I wanted to show you my new dress." She tried to twirl while holding on to the chair but only managed a slight swish of her dress. "Do you like it, Daddy?"

"It's nice. Now go back to your mother." Daddy joined his fellow musicians, fingering the worn frets and plucking his guitar.

Anna Joy's smile faded. Didn't Daddy think she looked pretty? She turned toward her room. Her eyes filled with tears.

"Hey, little lady, that's a mighty fine dress." The deep voice slurred. The man reached out his hand and grabbed at Anna Joy. But as she pulled away, his hand grasped the fabric of her dress. *Rip.*

Anna Joy gasped. Her pretty ruffle dangled from a beefy hand. She stared into the bloodshot eyes of a man laughing and holding a cigar between his yellowed teeth.

Frightened and embarrassed, she sought out her daddy with her eyes. Surely, he would help her. *Daddy, where are you?* A sob escaped her lips.

Her dad stumbled over. "Get used to it, kid," he slurred as he staggered out of the room, laughing.

Anna Joy crawled into the bedroom, sobbing.

Betty looked up from settling the baby and frowned at Anna Joy. "What happened to you? You tore your new dress."

"I didn't do it." Anna Joy choked out the words between sniffles. "Daddy's friend did."

Betty grasped Anna Joy's shoulders. "I told you to stay out of there."

Anna Joy slumped to the floor. *Where did my daddy go?* Daddy, who helped his Pumpkin to stand, pushed her in her pedal car, and carried her on his shoulders.

.·∽✺∾·.

"One of your lady friends showed up at my door today." Betty's eyes narrowed as she regarded her husband through a puff of cigarette smoke.

"What did she want?" Earl avoided her gaze, rooting in the refrigerator for a beer.

"Apparently, she wanted you. Funny how she didn't know or care that you had a wife and kids." Betty had heard the rumors about her husband and other women, but she'd brushed them aside, denying the truth she already suspected.

"I don't know what your problem is. We had a few drinks and some laughs. What am I supposed to do?" Earl said. "You never go out with me anymore."

"Well, maybe I'm a little busy taking care of your children. Anna Joy needs her therapy. I just can't walk out and leave them, Earl, like you do."

"Find a babysitter." Earl popped the cap and kicked the door shut. "It can't be all that hard."

Betty snorted. "You try finding a babysitter for a disabled child who spikes fevers at the drop of a hat and then has seizures."

Earl stomped into the living room, brushing past Anna Joy's outstretched arms.

Betty called after him. "I won't tolerate another woman, Earl."

.ᵕ᎒ᵕ.

It wasn't long before Betty decided to do something about Earl's wandering eye.

"But Daddy, aren't you coming?" Anna Joy said.

"You're better off with your mother, Pumpkin," her dad said as he lifted her into the back seat of the car and closed the door. He stood in the driveway with his hands in his pockets as Anna Joy, her mother, and Earl Junior drove away.

"I want my daddy! I want my daddy!" Anna Joy sobbed. She pressed her tear-stained face against the rear window; hands stretched toward her daddy's retreating form. Then he disappeared.

Betty had packed her children and what little else she could into the car—leaving Earl—and drove north to live with her family. She soon filed divorce papers.

3.

Auntie and Uncle

God places the lonely in families.

Psalm 68:6 (NLT)

The dusky skies somewhat hid Betty's tear-stained cheeks as she pulled into the driveway at her sister's home. She hoped this arrangement would work out. The house seemed awfully small for five children. She pried her fingers loose from the steering wheel. She hadn't realized how tightly she was clinging to the wheel. Her muscles felt tight and stiff as she turned to step out of the vehicle. Betty reached for her two-year-old son, sleeping in the back seat.

Her sister draped her arm around Betty and led her back into the house. "Let me help you get settled."

Uncle wrapped his arms around Anna Joy and carried her inside. "Here's my little girl!" He grinned at Anna Joy and settled her on the couch. He returned to the car, gathered Betty's belongings, and carried them into the spare bedroom. On his way back to the living room, he retrieved his hairbrush, walked over to Anna Joy, and smiled. "Would you like to brush my hair? I don't have a little girl to brush my hair for me. Will you be my little girl?"

Anna Joy nodded.

Uncle handed her the hairbrush and slipped onto the floor in front of her, resting his back against the sofa. Somehow, Uncle knew that this little girl needed a daddy in her life.

Anna Joy clumsily wrapped her fingers around the brush handle and stroked Uncle's wavy black hair. Brushing his thick hair would become their tradition.

.·ᢀᢒᢀ·.

Anna Joy looked forward to her uncle coming home at the end of the week. The aroma of roast beef and mashed potatoes permeated the house, a real treat from ketchup sandwiches. Uncle sat at the head of the table, and everyone understood that he served himself first, the best of the roast. Auntie had said, "Your uncle is the main breadwinner of this family, and he needs to keep up his strength." He drove a semi to support his wife and three boys.

Auntie disciplined with the occasional deserved swat on the behind, but Uncle never spanked. He played, wrestling with the boys and tickling Anna Joy. No hitting was allowed, especially hitting Anna Joy even if she instigated the scuffle. "Boys do not hit girls," Uncle said. "Ever."

Auntie babysat for Betty, who waitressed in the evening in addition to her day job.

.·ᢀᢒᢀ·.

One evening when Anna Joy's mom was working and Auntie had plans, Uncle watched the children. He had tucked them in for the night. Anna Joy and her brother shared a double bed with their mother. Her cousins bunked in the next room. Uncle settled into his lounge chair and lifted the footrest. Now he could listen to simultaneous ball games on several radio stations. He enjoyed keeping track of each player, inning, and score.

He didn't know that the children had made a pact. "Let's see if we can get Dad to spank us!" someone had said. They laughed, giggled, and knocked on the wall between their rooms.

Uncle waited to see if they would settle before dropping the footrest and hoisting himself out of his chair. He opened each bedroom door. "Settle down, now. It's time to go to sleep." He padded back down the hall, plopped in his chair, and put his feet up.

As he tuned back in to the baseball games, he heard squeals of laughter bubbling out into the hallway. Once again, he got up and lumbered down the hall. The room exploded in giggles as a pillow landed at his feet. "If you don't settle down, I'll have to spank you." A pained look crossed his face.

Uncle returned to his games and chair. Ruckus from the bedrooms escalated. He strode into the bedrooms and landed a light swat on each bottom buried beneath layers of covers. "Now go to sleep."

.·ৎ৩ৎ·.

Anna Joy whimpered. Not from the spanking itself because she could barely feel the swat, but she couldn't believe Uncle would spank her. They had accomplished their goal. But she wasn't sure what hurt more, the spanked bottoms or her uncle's disappointment in their disobedience.

"Which one of you broke the lamp?" Auntie said the next morning in a controlled tone. She lined up the five children, attempting to screen the culprit. She crossed her arms and tapped her foot. "I'm asking one last time. Who broke the lamp? If you don't tell me, I'll punish all of you."

Her gaze met silent, downcast faces.

Auntie grabbed a switch.

Anna Joy trailed after the boys, squealing and running as fast as her crutches and knee-length braces allowed. She didn't dare glance back. She knew Auntie wasn't far behind.

But Anna Joy abided by the family code: you never ratted on each other. Of course, that meant she often got spanked for something she never did. Auntie caught her first and grew too tired to continue the chase. Today would be no different. But a code was a code. Anna Joy didn't mind taking the lickings for the others. All for one and one for all.

Anna Joy and the boys had been playing cowboys and Indians, whooping, hollering, and tearing through the house. They crawled over, around, and through the blankets and cushions of their makeshift forts. She wasn't sure who broke the lamp.

One rule they never broke. After Auntie cleaned the house on Fridays, she demanded thirty minutes to admire her efforts before the child tornado spawned a muddy path through her kitchen.

On cleaning day, Anna Joy grabbed her doll, deposited it in the full-size baby buggy, and pursued the boys as they rode their bikes up and down the street. Unknown to her at the time, the doctor had instructed her mother to weight the carriage with a twenty-five-pound bag of flour. Pushing the buggy was part of her therapy since the flour would stabilize the unit and strengthen Anna Joy's walking muscles.

She enjoyed pushing her little carriage, especially when she caught one of the cats, dressed it up like a baby doll, and wrapped a blanket around the squirming kitty. Once tucked in, the cat yowled his displeasure, wriggled out of the blanket, and leaped out of the buggy.

Eventually, Anna Joy acquired a three-wheel therapy bike. No longer hampered by her hindrance, she squealed, "I'm free! I'm free!" She sped after her brother and cousins. "I'll race you!"

Auntie watched from the porch. "You can only ride on our street."

.ɔ৹৫ɔ.

One day Anna Joy decided to ride her bike around the block all by herself. A group of boys blocked her path and yanked her off her tricycle. Anna Joy grasped her crutches and trudged toward home, sobbing.

Her cousin Jimmy, a few years younger, caught up with her, "What happened? Where's your bike?"

"I was just riding around the block." She sniffled.

"You know you're not supposed to ride on that street. It's not safe." He dashed into the house and returned, wielding a baseball bat. He marched down the street and disappeared around the block.

A short time later, he reappeared, pedaling Anna Joy's bike. He stopped in front of her. "They won't bother you again. But stay off their street."

Auntie set ketchup sandwiches and Kool-Aid out on the picnic table for lunch. Neither Jimmy nor Anna Joy told her of their morning adventures. Auntie turned to Anna Joy. "We're out of milk for the baby. I need to borrow some money from you." Money was tight even with Uncle's income and Anna Joy's mom working two jobs. Child support was nearly non-existent. Auntie knew the few coins accumulated by the boys were spent as quickly as received. But Anna Joy carefully tucked her coins away.

She pulled out her meager savings, mostly birthday money she had stashed in her drawer, and counted out the milk money. She knew Auntie would never pay her back. There was never any extra money. But that was ok. This was what you did when you were family.

The family rarely had fresh fruit in the house except at Christmas when they received a large orange in their Christmas stockings. One day, Anna Joy wanted a big juicy peach. But there was one problem. She was not allowed to cross the two busy streets by herself to go to the grocery store. She glanced around the house. Auntie was nowhere in sight. She slid the drawer open, grabbed her money, and slipped out the door, closing it ever so slowly so it wouldn't slam.

Tapping the pavement with her crutches, one after the other, she sashayed to the corner, crossed the two busy streets, and entered the store. She balanced herself against the produce case, squeezing one peach after another until she picked out the most sumptuous peach she could find. At the register, she counted out her coins and plunked them on the counter.

Juice slid down her chin as she leaned against the store window, savoring her peach. She knew she would get in trouble, and if she didn't finish her peach in the store, Auntie would confiscate it and make her share her prized fruit. Anna Joy knew the rules. All treats were shared, even if purchased with your own money.

Proud of herself, Anna Joy sauntered toward the street corner. She looked up at the stoplight and spotted Auntie across the street, arms crossed, cheeks puffed out. Auntie grabbed Anna Joy's arm. "You know better than to cross the street."

She allowed Auntie to lead her home. The mouth-watering peach would be worth the spanking.

4.

Faith of a Child

But Jesus said, "Let the little children come to Me, and do
not forbid them; for of such is the kingdom of heaven."

Matthew 19:14 (NKJV)

Anna Joy peeked around the corner. Several not-so-gentle snores reverberated down the hall. The adults had retreated to their bedrooms for Sunday afternoon naps. The coast was clear. She scooted into the living room, flipped the dial on the black-and-white television, and turned the volume to low. The snoring stopped. She paused, holding her breath.

The snores resumed. *Phew!*

She crawled a few feet away from the TV, turned around, and rotated her legs out to either side in a W-sitting position. She couldn't understand why the adults got so mad and spanked her when she sat in her favorite position. The doctor had said something about tightness in her leg muscles, making it more difficult for her to walk. But she felt proud of herself for being able to sit up without support.

Strains from the program's theme song drifted into the living room. She loved listening to this man who preached and prayed for people. But Anna Joy knew if one of the adults woke before the miracle service ended, she would get doubly spanked.

The first time Auntie caught her, she swatted Anna Joy's bottom and said, "We don't watch that kind of program in this house. He doesn't practice our religion. Do you understand?"

"Yes, Auntie." But she really didn't understand. What was wrong with watching a man pray for people to get better?

Anna Joy swept aside the threats of punishment as the program began. The man in a suit stood in front of the microphone, held a black Bible, and gestured passionately as he spoke about Jesus. Her eyes widened as the television cameras spanned the crowd. There must be hundreds of people filling the tent! Men and women decked out in their Sunday best.

"Now I'm going to pray for the sick. God is the healer. I am not," the man said. "These people come from all walks of life to be healed. I'm going to pray for them. While I pray for them, if you'll believe right there in your home, God will heal you too."

Anna Joy leaned forward, her eyes fixed on the man sitting on the folding chair. A line of people wound around the perimeter of the tent. As each person approached him, they handed him a card with their name and prayer need. Then the man laid his hands on the people, their heads, or other parts of their bodies. One man heard a pop in his ear and said he could hear. Between sobs, a little boy said he could see. She watched a huge lump disappear from a woman's neck.

"God can heal you in your home," the man said. "If you want to be healed, put your hand on the part of your body you want healed. Or as a point of contact, place your hand on the television screen."

Anna Joy rested her hands on her legs, closed her eyes, and heard him pray, "Heal every person in this room from the crown of their heads to the soles of their feet. Lord, heal crippled limbs, deaf ears, and blind eyes! Now raise your hands and praise him."

Anna Joy raised her little hands and prayed, "Jesus, heal me." The program ended. She lowered her hands, scooted over to the television set, and turned the dial.

Maybe someday.

5.

First Communion

When we bless the cup at the Lord's Table, aren't we
sharing in the blood of Christ? And when we break the
bread, aren't we sharing in the body of Christ?

1 Corinthians 10:16 (NLT)

T *ap, tap, tap* broke the silence. Heads turned as the sound resonated throughout the vaulted ceiling of the ornate Catholic church. Congregants peered around alabaster pillars, staring at the little girl as she hobbled up the long marble aisle. Her white dress swished around her knee-length braces. A lacy veil fluttered over her forearms, partially concealing the cuff of her crutches. Women with veiled hats smiled and dabbed their eyes with dainty handkerchiefs.

Today was Anna Joy's special day—her First Holy Communion.

She had prepared for First Communion all year long under the tutelage of Sister Mark. The nun spoke few words, but Anna Joy loved her. Sister Mark radiated the love of Jesus.

"Jesus, I want to belong to you like Sister Mark does," Anna Joy prayed at the end of her First Communion preparation. "I want to belong to you spirit, soul, and body."

The day finally arrived when she would be deemed worthy enough to receive the body and blood of Jesus—her First Holy Communion. She sat in the pew, gazing at the crucifix above the altar, and said, "Jesus, come and be my friend."

She heard Jesus say, "All right." It was the first time she heard his voice. He came into her heart.

The priest, clothed in an elaborate vestment, faced the white marble altar that seemed to expand all the way to the ceiling. Robed altar boys flanked him, their backs to the congregation. Since the priest prayed in Latin, she understood little of what he said, but she had dutifully memorized the proper Latin responses.

The priest raised the Host above his head. The altar boy rang the chimes. Then the priest raised the chalice, and once again, the chimes reverberated throughout the church. The consecration was complete. The Host was now Jesus's body, the wine his blood.

Anna Joy's stomach rumbled. She licked her dry lips. She'd had nothing to eat or drink after midnight, as was required by the church prior to receiving the Eucharist. She ignored these trite discomforts in joyful anticipation of receiving Jesus, being united with him. Her first step to being like Sister Mark.

The rap of a crutch preceded each step toward the altar. She knelt at the marble communion rail.

The altar boy rested one hand over his heart and, with the other, extended the golden plate beneath her chin. Sister Mark had told her that the Host must never fall to the floor.

The priest held the Host up with his stubby fingers. "The body of Christ."

Anna Joy opened her mouth and stuck out her tongue.

The priest placed the unleavened bread on her tongue and proceeded to the next recipient.

She held the wafer in her mouth until it dissolved as she had been instructed. You never bit or chewed the body of Christ.

Back home, she received the traditional First Communion gifts.

Carefully, she paged through her new white leather prayer book. She pulled her white rosary out of its case and fingered each bead. Just like Sister Mark's.

.ཕ஭ఠ.

Many years later, Anna Joy's seven-year-old goddaughter twirled around Anna Joy's room in her lacy white First Communion dress and veil.

Anna Joy bubbled over with joy as she remembered her First Holy Communion—walking up the aisle in her white dress and veil—symbolizing her new relationship with Christ as his bride.

They sat on the bedroom floor together. Anna Joy took a sheet of notebook paper and a pen and drew two houses side-by-side.

"The big house is Jesus's house, and the little house is your house." She pointed to the big house and then the smaller house. "You can go to Jesus's house anytime you like." She drew a path from the little house to the big house. "When you receive Holy Communion"—she traced the path from Jesus's house to her god-daughter's house—"Jesus comes to live in your house forever."

6.

Foster Fiasco

He delivered me from my strong enemy, From those
who hated me, For they were too strong for me.

Psalm 18:17 (NKJV)

"Your daughter may benefit from a special school for the handicapped," the doctor said, glancing at Anna Joy. "They have classes in the morning and therapy in the afternoon. This may be a good way for her to receive the intensive physical therapy she needs to walk."

"But the school is so far away," Betty said. "I'm not sure how I'd get her there with working two jobs."

"We could provide a foster care situation."

"Like a foster home?" Mom pursed her lips like she did when she was mad. "I can't afford that."

"You wouldn't have to pay for it. The state would pick up the tab."

Betty paused and studied Anna Joy. "She would get the therapy and the education she needs?"

"Of course!" The doctor smiled.

.ﮨﮩﮬ.

Anna Joy sat on their bed, her crossed eyes watching her mom pack her few belongings in a battered suitcase. "Are we going somewhere, Mommy?"

"You're going to go to a special school," Betty said, her voice quavering. "You'll learn a lot, and they'll even help you walk." She smiled. "You'll be living with a new family while you're going to school."

Later that day, Betty placed the suitcase in the trunk. She turned toward her daughter with a tear in her eye, "It's time to go."

Anna Joy climbed into the car and settled herself next to the window. She pressed her face to the glass as they wound along country roads, passing farmland and towns. She only half-listened to her mother's reassurances that this move was for her own good.

When they finally arrived, Anna Joy trailed her mom as she walked up to the door. The house seemed friendly enough—kids toys strewn across the lawn. Mom rang the doorbell.

A woman opened the door. "Come on in." She wiped her hands on her apron. "I'm just starting dinner." The odor of cooked onions and peppers wafted into the living room. She yelled for one of her children. "Show her to her room." She pointed toward Anna Joy.

Betty and Anna Joy followed the child to a dimly lit room with barely enough space to fit a twin bed and a dresser. As Anna Joy sat down on the edge of the bed, the springs creaked. Mom unpacked the suitcase, carefully folding the clothes and laying them in the drawer. She hung a few items in the narrow closet.

"As long as she does what she's told, we'll get along just fine." The foster mother placed her hands on her hips as she surveyed Anna Joy.

Mom cupped her daughter's face in her hands and kissed her on the forehead. "You be a good girl, now." A tear trickled down Betty's cheek as she turned to leave.

Later, Anna Joy heard the lock click on her bedroom door for the night.

Night after night, she licked her dry lips, but she knew better than to drink any liquids after supper.

.₰₰.

"Here, kitty, kitty!" Anna Joy coaxed the cat to come out from under her bed.

"Meow."

Once again, he had slipped in before the door was locked for the night. She shivered and caressed the kitty as she slid beneath the ragged blanket.

Cuddling the kitty provided a welcome distraction from the rumbling in her belly. Her dinner—a scoop of leftover rice and a hard crust of bread—failed to satisfy her hunger.

Her foster mother's words echoed in her mind. "The meat and potatoes are for the family and not the likes of you."

Hungry, Anna Joy had quietly eaten her meager dinner. Once again, she had pitched her daily lunch. The thick surplus bologna sandwich and a wormy apple landed in the trash at the school for children with disabilities. She hated bologna.

.₰₰.

Excitement welled up in Anna Joy in anticipation of her mom's visit. She quickly slipped into her dress. The dress seemed looser. *Who let out the seams?*

When Mom arrived, she placed her hands on Anna Joy's shoulders. "How's my best girl? Are you getting enough to eat?"

Anna Joy nodded. She didn't want to make any trouble. She knew her foster mother was within earshot.

"You look thinner." Betty smiled. "It must be all that extra therapy they're having you do at the school. You're just getting stronger. You'll be able to walk without your crutches soon."

Anna Joy stared at her scuffed shoes, silent.

When her mom arrived the next month, Anna Joy mustered

her happy face as she walked out to meet her. Her dress hung loosely around her shoulders, swishing below her leg braces.

Betty gasped. "I don't know what you're giving her to eat," she said to the foster mother. "But obviously it's not enough. Look at her!" She huffed and pointed toward Anna Joy.

"We're going home," Betty said. She stomped into Anna Joy's room, ripped her clothes off the hangers, and tossed her belongings into the suitcase. "Somehow, we'll work it out so you can stay in the handicap school and get the therapy you need."

7.

The Orthopedic School

Commit yourself to instruction; listen
carefully to words of knowledge.

Proverbs 23:12 (NLT)

"Out of all the children in the orthopedic school, the county Easterseals committee selected you, Anna Joy, to be our Easterseals poster child."[1]

With nut-brown ringlets framing her face, Anna Joy posed next to the Easterseals poster with its traditional lily logo with the tagline HELP CRIPPLED CHILDREN. Her grin revealed a missing tooth. The ruffled dress overshadowed her below-the-knee braces as it fanned out along the line of her wooden crutches.

At a tea for Easterseals volunteers, Anna Joy perched on the edge of a buffet, charming donors with her winsome smile. Maybe the committee had spotted the spunk and determination emanating from this good-natured seven-year-old. Donors sealed envelopes with the Easterseals stamp, reminding others to help disabled children live normal lives.

---

1   In 2016, Easter Seals changed its name to Easterseals. "Easter Seals Is Now Easterseals In National Rebranding," *The Non Profit Times*, May 3, 2016, accessed September 4, 2025, https://thenonprofittimes.com/npt_articles/easter-seals-now-easterseals-national-rebranding/.

The orthopedic school provided a combination of class work and therapy: physical, occupational, and speech. Anna Joy often grimaced and arched her back off the mat as the therapist stretched her leg muscles. She didn't know whether to scream from the painful stretching in her calf or cry out in relief as the charley horses gripping her muscles unknotted.

Anna Joy's best friend, born with muscular dystrophy, provided a welcome distraction from the monotony of therapy. One such distraction came when it was her turn to lie on the mat while the therapist performed passive range of motion exercises on her legs.

Across the room, Anna Joy grasped the parallel bars and shuffled to the end, belting out, "One hundred bottles of beer on the wall..."[2]

Soon her bestie joined in, "Take one down, pass it around, ninety-nine bottles of beer on the wall."

In seventh grade, a new girl enrolled in the orthopedic school. Along with the rest of her classmates, Anna Joy's friend gravitated toward the new girl, shutting out Anna Joy. In the lunchroom, she sat alone at the table, tears spilling onto her sandwich. Stifled giggles from whispered secrets drifted toward her ears.

In the therapy room, a chorus of "99 Bottles of Beer" no longer rang out. Anna Joy plodded between the metal bars in a silence broken only by her therapist's instructions. Across the room, snickers from shared secrets between best friends triggered another stream of tears for Anna Joy.

For eighth grade, she transferred to a regular school. She couldn't bear standing on the outside staring into a world that not only no longer welcomed her but also ostracized her from friendship. Besides, she had read most of the books in the library.

---

2 Traditional folk song, "99 Bottles of Beer on the Wall," lyrics and melody in the public domain.

8.

A Surgeon's Promise

For he has not ignored or belittled the suffering of the needy. He has not turned his back on them, but has listened to their cries for help.

Psalm 22:24 (NLT)

"If we do these surgeries," the doctor said as he leaned back on his stool, "I promise you, your daughter will walk."

"She'll really walk?" Betty's eyes widened. "No braces or crutches?"

"Oh yes! The tendons in her legs have shortened and are too tight," the surgeon said. "We'll cut the tendons in her legs, releasing those muscles so she will be able to plant her foot flat on the ground and walk normally instead of dragging her foot."

Betty regarded her young daughter, noting her legs imprisoned by braces and her arms shackled by crutches dangling from her tiny wrists.

Anna Joy watched her mom through the thick glasses that had been prescribed to correct her crossed-eyed vision.

Mom pursed her lips. "We'll do the surgery."

·୬ଡ଼୭·

Anna Joy attempted to roll over, but waves of pain tore through her legs and competed with the nausea roiling in her belly. *Why do my legs feel so heavy, stiff?* She moaned. *Where am I?* Then she remembered Mom had told her she was going to the hospital. Something about surgery—her legs. *Oh, that's why they hurt!*

"I think she's waking up." A brusque voice penetrated the inky blackness surrounding her. Someone ripped off her covers. Anna Joy shivered.

She struggled to open her eyes, weighted down by drugged sleep. Through a blurred haze, she saw a woman clad in white bending over her, grasping the bar between her knees. Jolt! Searing pain pulsated throughout her legs. She cried out. Her eyes shot open.

"That's better now," the nurse said. "It's good to see you awake."

Anna Joy scanned the room. *One, two, three . . . seven beds.* "Where's my mom?"

"Your mama's not here right now. She had to leave. You were sleeping. Visiting hours are over for the day." She patted Anna Joy's arm. "We'll take good care of you. You be a good girl now."

The blackness of night closed in, but the ensuing darkness failed to block the cries of the other children or the screams of the little boy with third-degree burns wrapped in white bandages. She wrinkled her nose as the stench of burned flesh, excrement, and bodily fluids permeated the air.

Dark nights in foster care had steeled her for being alone. At least then, the cat had slipped through the door before her foster mother locked her in the attic room after supper. Cuddling the kitty had provided a distraction from the growling in her belly.

But there was no kitty for her to cuddle in the children's ward, and listening to the whimpers of the other children proved worse than being alone.

Hopefully her mom would come soon and pull her out of the hospital like she did with foster care.

.⁓ℓℯ⁓.

"My legs burn. Take the casts off!" Anna Joy pleaded with her mom, tears rolling down her cheeks. Her mom could only come during visiting hours, a few hours the hospital designated during the afternoon.

"The casts will help you walk." Betty tried to encourage her daughter.

"I don't care! They hurt!" She wiggled to reach her fingers into the cast to scratch the incessant itch.

Her mom gasped when she pulled back the sheets. Angry red blisters blanketed Anna Joy's legs from her casts to her groin. Mom called for the nurse.

"This isn't normal!" Betty crossed her arms and frowned.

The nurse pulled back the covers. "Oh my!" She dashed out of the room.

A few minutes later, she returned, a doctor trailing behind.

"She's allergic to the casts. We'll have to take them off immediately." He turned to the nurse. "We'll need gauze bandages and salve." He left the room and returned with the cast cutter.

The nurse juggled salve and an armload of gauze, dumping them on the bedside table. She shooed Betty out of the room and pulled the flimsy curtain around Anna Joy's bed.

The whir of the blades thrummed in Anna Joy's ears as the saw penetrated the plaster cast. She gritted her teeth and stiffened. Finally, the casts fell away, revealing blisters comparable to third-degree burns. A putrid odor wafted toward her nostrils. Anna Joy howled as the nurse lifted her legs one at a time so the doctor could slather the thick cream on her excoriated limbs and wrap them with gauze.

After they finished, Anna Joy relaxed and slept for a few hours. The searing pain in her legs only slightly dulled.

.⁓ℓℯ⁓.

Oh no, not again! It wasn't her fault. But she knew the nurse would yell at her. She'd called for the bedpan as soon as she knew she had to go. But they didn't come soon enough. They never did. Anna Joy hoped the nurse who scrubbed her so roughly during her bath wasn't the one who answered the call light. The nurses didn't like having to change her bed or the gauze bandages more than once a day.

That surgery was only the beginning of Anna Joy's progress. With each surgery, the doctors promised Betty that Anna Joy would walk.

Once home, she trained her cat to pad up and down over her itchy scars. His claws penetrated the gauze bandages in just the right places.

After each surgery, Anna Joy continued walking with crutches, dragging her foot, and scraping the toe of her shoe. The only difference was multiple scars and damaged nerves.

She wore the knee-length braces until one day, her mother intervened. "Even though these braces cost a lot of money, they are not helping you walk." She unbuckled the straps, removed the braces along with the orthopedic shoes attached with a strip of metal, and tossed the braces into the trash.

No more orthopedic shoes!

9.

The Stepfather

The LORD is my rock, my fortress, and my savior;
my God is my rock, in whom I find protection.

Psalm 18:2 (NLT)

Anna Joy stole a glance toward the door before scanning the perimeter of the kitchen. She hoped the faded carpet in the rickety trailer would absorb the *thump thump* of her crutches.

"You're not going anywhere," her stepfather growled, his back toward her. He scooped a stack of pancakes off the griddle and tossed them on a plate.

"Eat!" He slammed the plate on the table.

She froze. Not the pancakes again. So close and yet so far. A few more steps and she would've been out the door. The oily, sweet odor of pancakes filled her nostrils. Her stomach roiled.

He grabbed her arms, swiveled her around, and shoved her into the chair.

She tried to squirm away but stopped when she spotted the chip in the kitchen sink and remembered the crash followed by her mom's screams. Anna Joy's stepfather had slammed her mother's body against the sink. A slow construction season had not improved his temper.

He snatched the fork, stabbed the uncut pancake, and thrust the greasy mash into her mouth.

Gagging, she turned her head and tried to swipe his hand away, but his grip was too strong.

"Are you going to eat them by yourself, or do I have to force-feed you?" He sneered as he poked the fork at her face. "I'll make you so fat that no one will want you." He snarled at her, curling his lip. "If I can't have you, then no one else will have you either!" The fork clanked as he slammed it on the table.

Her fingers trembled as she picked up the fork. Watching him out of the corner of her eye, she choked down the pancakes. After rinsing her plate, she slipped the strap of her school bag over her shoulder, grasped her crutches, and stepped outside. Breathe. Gritting her teeth, Anna Joy curled her fingers around the stair rail. The morning sun had already scorched the metal, which seared the palm of her hand. She yanked her long sleeves down. No one could see her bruises. After rounding the corner, out of sight of the trailer, she threw up the pancakes. She hated pancakes.

Anna Joy understood why her mother wanted to remarry. Working two jobs to support her children and making decisions by herself had ultimately worn Betty down. She met her new husband while working as a cocktail waitress. He was a regular and had taken a shine to her, pursuing her until she agreed to marry him.

As a freshman in high school, Anna Joy finally had her own bed in the trailer. Her new room, separated from her brother's by a thin plywood wall, barely fit a twin bed. But she no longer had to feign sleep while lying in the double bed with her mother and brother as her mom sobbed into her pillow, missing her ex-husband.

Anna Joy not only acquired a stepfather but a new home far away from Auntie and her cousins. How she wished she could still live with her aunt. She missed Auntie and her family, especially Jimmy, her protector.

One day Jimmy drove into the trailer park and rapped on the door.

"Jimmy! What are you doing here?" Anna Joy could hardly contain her enthusiasm as she stepped out and hugged her cousin. "Did you really drive here? You don't even have a license!"

"I know how to drive. Don't you remember me driving Dad's big rig when I was nine? Boy, I sure got a whuppin' for that! Besides, can't I come visit my favorite cousin?"

Anna Joy's stepfather walked out, slamming the door. "What are you doing out here, you lazy tramp!" He grabbed Anna Joy's arms and yanked her off the stoop.

"Hey, you don't talk to her like that!" Jimmy stood up and balled his fists.

Anna Joy's eyes widened, and she shook her head at Jimmy.

"You don't tell me what to do in my house! You going to fight me, boy?" He threw back his head and laughed.

Jimmy raised his fists and lunged toward the man. But before Jimmy could throw a punch, Anna Joy's stepfather grabbed him by the collar and tossed him down the steps.

"Jimmy!" Anna Joy cried, stumbling toward him. She glanced back to her stepfather as he stepped back into the trailer.

"I'm okay," Jimmy said as he got up off the ground. "I guess I'd better go. You be careful now, you hear?" He drove away—his first and last visit.

.⟶⟵.

Once, after her bath, Anna Joy sat on the floor of the tiny bathroom, grabbed her towel, and started drying off. She felt the door bump her behind. She stiffened and wrapped the towel tightly around her. Blocked by her body, the door could open only a few inches. As the heavy footsteps faded away, she heard muttered curses.

Later, in the middle of the night, she jerked awake. An icy presence towered over her. Facing the wall, she pulled her cat tight to her chest. *Don't move!* The foul odor of stale beer and cigarette smoke wafted over her with each heavy breath. Her body tensed. She held her breath. If she lay perfectly still, maybe he would leave.

Soon she heard the creaking of floorboards as the footsteps shuffled down the hall. She took a deep breath and snuggled her kitty. The kitty wasn't supposed to be in her bed. If he had found her cat, the brute would have drowned him.

He wouldn't be back tonight.

10.

High School Compadres

He led me to a place of safety; he rescued
me because he delights in me.

Psalm 18:19 (NLT)

The principal tapped his pencil on the desk and studied Anna Joy.

She held her breath. What if he said no?

"Can you manage to get yourself between our two buildings at least once a day?"

"I'll sure try!"

He smiled. "If you can stand it, so can we." He pulled out the registration papers and handed her a pen. "Welcome to our school."

"Yes!" Anna Joy cried out and clapped her hands. She took the pen and filled out the forms. As she signed her name, she paused mid-signature, remembering her stepfather's words, "You'll only go to school under my name, and my name will be the surname on your diploma."

She resumed penning her signature, dutifully scrawling his name. But even her stepfather's demand could not diminish her excitement. Now it was official—she would be a real high school freshman.

.ᗝⴹᴐ.

Anna Joy couldn't wait to get to school on her first day of classes. Her hunger for learning and real high school experiences trumped the rumbling in her stomach. She stared at the two buildings, their stacked rows of windows towering over her. Lots of classrooms, and lots of stairs. She adjusted her bookbag, bulging with her new textbooks—English, algebra, world history, science, and Latin—grabbed the rail, and climbed the concrete steps.

She entered the building, scanning the long hall lined with lockers punctuated by scratched wooden classroom doors. An isolated wheelchair stood off to the side. She wrinkled her nose. Not so much from the musty old school odors, but the thought of being relegated to a wheelchair. She would walk with her crutches, thank you very much!

"Let me help you with your books," one girl said. "I'm Donna. We're in class together."

"And I'm Sandy," another girl said.

"Thanks!" Anna Joy smiled at them. Her first friends.

Donna and Sandy accompanied Anna Joy up several flights of stairs to their classroom.

.⦿ℓ⦿.

All of her therapy in the orthopedic school hadn't prepared Anna Joy for the first few weeks of classes—walking the maze of halls and trudging up and down multiple flights of stairs. By the end of the school day, her shoulder muscles ached, and her legs cramped. At night, she buried her face in the pillow, gritting her teeth to muffle her screams. *I can do this!* The last thing she wanted was to awaken her stepfather and give him the satisfaction of mocking her defeat.

Eventually her muscles adjusted to the rigors of high school. Her mother claimed that all of her walking at school had fostered the success of her bilateral knee surgeries performed to straighten her legs, even though two years had passed since her last surgery.

.ᴏᴈℰ⌃.

One morning, Anna Joy and her friends left the classroom together and headed for the stairs, stifling giggles. The girls had been allowed to leave the classroom ten minutes early to avoid the rush between classes. Anna Joy grabbed the rail and stepped down. Her foot slipped. She tumbled down the stairs.

Donna screamed.

Sandy raced down the stairs and bent over Anna Joy. "Are you okay?" Her voice quavered.

Anna Joy looked around, checked herself for injuries, and attempted a smile. "I'm okay." Donna and Sandy collected her crutches, helped her up, and brushed off her coat. Even though this wasn't her first fall, she felt humiliated by her lack of coordination and muscle control. Thankfully, no one else had seen her mishap. The subsequent bruises would appear later and merge with the rest of the purple and green blotches hidden beneath her clothing. Courtesy of her stepfather.

The orthopedic school did prepare her for one thing. Falls. Under the tutelage of her therapists, she had practiced over and over how to tumble so as not to break any bones.

Her therapist had said, "It's not a matter of if you fall, but when."

The rain had been beating on the windows all morning. Not a pleasant day to have to walk between buildings. Donna grabbed the wheelchair. Anna Joy threw her a disgusted look but gave in to her insistence. Donna pushed the wheelchair while Sandy held the door open and then carried her books across the quad to their next class. Anna Joy crossed between the two buildings at least once a day, but some days she made the trip several times.

Mr. Stevens taught world history and was one of her favorite teachers. One day he said, "I know the lunchroom can get pretty rowdy and crowded, so you're welcome to invite a friend or two to come have lunch in my classroom."

She accepted his invitation, along with her friends, and they became regulars in Mr. Stevens's makeshift lunchroom. She enjoyed their camaraderie and friendly banter.

One day, Anna Joy's friends were unable to join her in Mr. Stevens's classroom.

"Things aren't going so well at home, are they?" Mr. Stevens said.

Anna Joy refused to meet his gaze. "What do you mean?"

"No one comes to school in hot weather wearing long sleeves unless they have something to hide."

Anna Joy didn't answer but continued unpacking her lunch.

"Is he hitting you?"

"He gets upset sometimes." She looked down at her shoes. "He's just had trouble finding work."

"If you need to talk, my door is always open."

.ᴏଓᴇ.

Mr. Stevens proved to be not just a teacher but a friend. Anna Joy escaped to his house on weekends when her mother worked. Always a gentleman, he taught her about fashion, how a young lady should behave, and what a teenage girl needed to know about life because she had no one else to teach her. They worked puzzles, played cards and board games. Anna Joy loved to read, so they engaged in lively discussions about their favorite books and history. He provided her with a safe place.

Many years later, Anna Joy reminisced about Mr. Stevens with fondness. "He risked his job for me."

11.

A Praying Grandma

For you, God, have heard my vows; you have given
me the heritage of those who fear your name.

Psalm 61:5 (NIV)

A nna Joy's classmates poured out of the doors of the high school, whooping and hollering. She grinned, clinging to the stair rail while they flew past.

"What are you going to do over the summer?" Donna asked Anna Joy when the buzz died down.

"I'm going up north to my grandma's. I've spent every summer with her since I was six." She knew Mom sent her to Grandma Grace during the summer to protect her from her stepfather, a secret they never talked about.

"What do you do up there?"

"I help my grandma feed the chickens and collect eggs. In the evening, we sit on her porch and shell peas. She tells me stories about my mom and aunties when they were young and all the trouble they got into. My grandma has a rock driveway. When I was little, I'd sit in the rocks and look for all the pretty stones. Sometimes I'd find a pink rock sprinkled with crystals or a sparkly geode. Then I'd put them in a special box."

.ᴏꙅℓ℮ᴏ.

She paused, remembering the day the shadow of a man towered over her while she sifted through the rocks. She had looked up, shielding her eyes, but the glare of the sun blocked any recognition of the man's face.

"What are you doing here?" Grandma called out from the porch, glowering at the man, broom perched mid-sweep.

The man turned toward the porch, tossed a coin at Anna Joy's feet, and walked away.

Grandma stomped toward Anna Joy, broom in hand. She glared at the new car as it spun down the road.

"Who was that man, Grandma?"

"Your dad." Grandma turned and trudged back up to the porch. She grabbed her broom and swept with renewed vigor.

Anna Joy picked up the dime and turned it over in her fingers. She would add the shiny coin to her box of special rocks.

.ᴏꙅℓ℮ᴏ.

"Anna Joy, Anna Joy."

A hand was gently shaking her shoulder. She snuggled deeper under her cotton quilt. Grandma whispered her name again. Was it morning? She hadn't heard the rooster crow. She squinted, trying to adjust her eyes to the surrounding darkness.

"What time is it, Grandma?" she mumbled.

"It's three o'clock in the morning. Get up. Time to pray."

Anna Joy once again slipped out from under her covers and slid to the floor, joining her grandma on her knees.

Grandma fingered the beads of her rosary as she prayed in German. "I can't properly pray in English."

Anna Joy rested her head on the edge of the bed, intermittently jarring herself awake as Grandma prayed. With halting German, she mumbled the prayers with Grandma.

The sun peeked through the sheer curtains. The rooster crowed—6:00 a.m.

Grandma groaned as she pushed against the bed to raise herself from the floor. "You can go to bed now." Grandma padded into her bedroom and closed the door.

Anna Joy crawled into bed and pulled the covers over her head.

She awoke a few hours later, blinking in the sunlight streaming across her quilt. After dressing, she tiptoed into the kitchen so as not to awaken Grandma. A bowl of raspberries sat at Anna Joy's place on the table. She pulled the cream out of the refrigerator and poured a generous stream over the berries. Only at Grandma Grace's did she get berries and real cream.

12.

To Daddy's House

Every good and perfect gift is from above, coming
down from the Father of the heavenly lights, who
does not change like shifting shadows.

James 1:17 (NIV)

"Hi, Pumpkin!" A voice resonated through the phone.

Anna Joy had not heard that term of endearment for years. "Daddy!"

"How would you like to come out for a visit during your school break? I'll send you a plane ticket."

"I'd love to!" She shrieked, bouncing in her chair like a three-year-old, a reaction to happiness she never outgrew.

.ༀ.

Anna Joy craned her neck out the car window, the balmy wind blowing her hair. She loved the breezes on her face. She didn't care that her neck already felt strained. There had been so much to see on her first plane ride too. Bison and livestock had dotted the plains, which soon gave way to jagged mountain peaks, piercing the clouds. Finally the ocean, its waves crashing the shoreline.

"Now don't you go falling out that window." Dad glanced toward her. "There's plenty of time to see all the sights." He pulled into the driveway.

"Anna Joy, Anna Joy!" Little Janet and her big brother, Billy, rushed toward the doorway, nearly toppling her with their hugs. "We can't believe you're here! We thought we'd never get to see you!"

"I couldn't wait to meet you either. I'm so glad you invited me to come!"

"Come on! I want to show you my room." Eight-year-old Janet tugged at her arm.

"Me, too!" ten-year-old Billy chimed in.

"Be careful, you kids. Don't knock her over." Dad set her suitcases down inside the door. "Anna Joy, this is Ginnie." He gestured toward a woman standing in the kitchen doorway. A lacy apron graced the trim waist of a woman with perfectly coiffed hair. A strand of pearls circled her slim neck.

Anna Joy's breath caught in her throat. She had been told that her dad's second wife looked like a younger version of her mother, but she was not prepared for such a close resemblance.

"Hi, Anna Joy, we're so glad to have you here," Ginnie said. "Janet, can you show Anna Joy to her room? We hope that you will find our guest room comfortable. You'll have your own private bath. Dinner is at six."

"Ok, then you can come see my room." Janet grabbed the smaller suitcase.

Anna Joy trailed behind Janet. She nearly drooled when she spotted the largest stereo system she had ever seen. Racks of phonograph records of all the top country artists lined the wall, a few practically spilling out of their jackets. She loved music, the one thing she had in common with her dad.

"Here we are." Janet spun around, arms outstretched.

Anna Joy stared at the spacious bedroom that could almost contain every room in her stepfather's trailer. The room dwarfed the double bed accented with decorative pillows and shams. She walked to the bathroom door and peered in, gawking at the peach-colored bathtub and matching toilet. A gilded mirror hung above the gold fixtures on the vanity. Peach towels draped decorative towel bars, a luxury she had only seen in photographs.

"You can put your clothes in these drawers." Janet tapped the top of the bureau adjacent to a mirrored dresser. "I'll help you. But I want to show you my room first. Come on!" She waved Anna Joy toward the door.

Up the stairs and down the hall, Anna Joy followed Janet, who repeatedly looked back to see if she was still coming. Anna Joy stopped in the doorway and gasped.

A menagerie of stuffed animals covered the pink frilly bed and toy chest. Big cats, kittens, floppy-eared dogs, and Micky Mouse. A life-sized teddy bear perched in the corner. How she would've loved to have even one of these plush toys when she was eight years old. A lump lodged in her throat. She rubbed her hands over the fur of a stuffed Siamese cat, her favorite, never having stroked a stuffed animal so soft. She pursed her lips, holding back a sob. This should have been her childhood.

"Do you like my room? Here's my favorite doll. You pull the string, and she talks." Janet pulled the "chatty ring."

"I love you," the canned voice said.

"I love you too!" Janet hugged her doll and then tossed her on the bed.

Anna Joy swallowed her grief and smiled. She would never begrudge all these nice things her dad had provided for his new family. Even in this short time, she loved Janet and Billy.

.୭ৡৎ.

"Hurry up, Anna Joy!" Janet bounded down the stairs. "I can't wait to get to Disneyland! We can go on all my favorite rides."

"I'm coming!" Anna Joy loved amusement parks. As a child, her brother would lift her up onto the rides at the fair. After the first time she threw up, he had told her, "Be sure you scream! Then you won't get sick."

Anna Joy screamed as she steered her flying saucer, the precursor to bumper cars, around the rink, careening into Janet and Billy. After they plunged down a waterfall on the Pirates of the Caribbean, skeletons and pirates popped out, eliciting shrieks from the tourists. The Jungle Ride, train rides, and her favorite—roller coasters—filled the magical day. They were greeted by Micky Mouse, Donald Duck, Snow White, and the seven dwarfs. It was a small world after all.

.ᴏᴏᴄ.

One morning when Anna Joy came down for breakfast, Ginnie placed a plate with half a cantaloupe on the table.

"Should I cut this up so each of us can have some?"

"No, dear, that's all for you."

Anna Joy stared at the cantaloupe. She had never eaten this much melon all by herself. At Auntie's, the whole family split one melon eight ways. She scooped out a spoonful, savoring its sweetness. Between bites, she asked, "Will my dad be around today?"

Ginnie turned toward the sink and swished the silverware in the dish water. "No, dear. He's on his boat today."

"Are we going too?" With a parade of pictures, Dad had showed off his party-sized yacht. She had hoped he'd take her for a boat ride on the open seas. She loved boating. As a child, various organizations had sponsored boat rides for children with disabilities. She'd jumped at these opportunities, whether pontoon boats, duck boats, sailboats, or speed boats. Her brother used to lift her into a boat and row out into the lake until the DNR caught up with them and sent them back to shore because they had no life jackets.

"No. His parties aren't for families." She turned toward Anna Joy, twisting the towel in her hand. "Look, I knew what your dad was like when I married him. But I love him. He's never been happy with just one woman, and I've learned to live with that." She turned back toward the sink. "Your mom never could."

.ᴄᴏᴄᴏ.

"I'd like to buy you a present," Dad said one day. "What would you like, Pumpkin?"

Anna Joy treasured jewelry, especially rings. It was the one thing of beauty she could not break if she fell. "I'd like a jade ring." She loved the color green.

Later that day, Dad presented her with a velvet jewelry box. "For you, Pumpkin. I hope you like it. A little something to remember your visit."

Her fingers fumbled opening the box. She stared at the most beautiful ring she had ever seen. A forest-green marquise-shaped jade gemstone set in a scrolled gold band.

.ᴄᴏᴄᴏ.

She always cherished the gift of this visit with her dad. The first, and last. The jade ring, the only present he ever gave her, never left her finger.

13.

College Life

Anna Joy blew out a deep breath, a mixture of excitement and trepidation. The campus was small by college standards, but she would adjust to the extra walking and stairs. After all, she had managed the stairs in both of her high school buildings. She couldn't wait to crack open her textbooks, especially psychology and French.

.ᴐᴗᴇᴐ.

Anna Joy tapped her crutches down the sidewalk of the college campus after class. A woman in a fur coat strode toward her. She looked familiar. Anna Joy squinted. This woman was the mother of her best friend from the orthopedic school.

"Hi, Anna Joy. I'm glad I found you. My daughter is in your class." The woman dropped her gaze, wringing her perfectly manicured fingers. "She doesn't have any friends. Would you be her friend?"

Anna Joy bit her lower lip, attempting to stave off the memories, the jeers of rejection from the orthopedic school. "I haven't seen her. Are you sure we have classes together?"

"You probably didn't recognize her. She's in a motorized wheelchair."

Anna Joy mentally scanned the faces of her classmates. The eyes of her mind rested upon a girl twisted with contractures in a wheelchair. She was so thin Anna Joy could encircle the girl's upper arm between her thumb and forefinger. Could this be her friend from the orthopedic school?

"Please." A tear rolled down the mother's cheek. "She doesn't have much time."

"I'll be her friend," Anna Joy said. Her heart ached for her friend's mother, who had already lost two of her four children to muscular dystrophy.

The anguish from her friend's betrayal in the orthopedic school had spun a web of distrust around Anna Joy's heart. But she made sure her friend never knew the truth. Anna Joy befriended her childhood bestie as promised. They laughed and reminisced as Anna Joy walked with her to class, sat with her at lunch, and listened to her secrets.

Until one day, her friend was gone.

.ₒₒₗₑₒ.

Prom was approaching, and the girls at school clucked and tittered as they planned, decorated, and raved about their dresses. They teased Anna Joy about her lack of a date.

But Anna Joy's cousin Jimmy came to her rescue once again. "I'm taking you to prom." Even though Jimmy was several years younger and still in high school, he oozed masculinity. Girls of all ages had been chasing him since he was twelve. He was equally adept at responding to or snubbing their advances. "Don't you dare tell anyone I'm your cousin. Do you understand?"

"You don't have to do this."

"I know, but you're my favorite cousin, and no one is going to treat you like that. Besides, I'm going to enjoy making them jealous." He flashed a cocky smile.

On prom day, Anna Joy treated herself to an afternoon at the salon. The beautician spent three hours sweeping her waist-length hair into an updo. The creation resembled a shellacked sculpture held in place with a canister of hairspray and a multitude of bobby pins. Anna Joy donned her floor-length prom dress, admired her reflection in the mirror, and waited for her escort.

Jimmy arrived in his best suit with a corsage in hand. He was so handsome. Helping her into and out of the car, he treated her as if she were a fragile doll. He wrapped his arm around Anna Joy and paraded her into the room decorated with streamers. He led her to a table covered with a white linen tablecloth and pulled out her chair. After bringing her a glass of punch, he pulled his chair close and draped his arm around her shoulders.

Anna Joy noted her classmates casting glances and batting their eyelashes at her striking escort.

But he focused his gaze on her.

"Would you like to dance?" A coy voice interrupted the strains of music flowing from the stage.

"I'm with her," Jimmy coolly replied, barely allowing his eyes to scan her beauty.

"Well, she certainly can't dance with you."

"I'm with her." He refused to meet her gaze as he focused his charming smile on Anna Joy.

After the girl strutted away, Anna Joy said, "I don't mind if you want to dance with the other girls."

"I'm not here to dance with them. I'm with you. They won't give you any more trouble."

.⟨∾⟩.

At the height of the Vietnam conflict, Jimmy had one dream—to be a Marine.

At age seventeen, he enlisted. The night before Jimmy left for boot camp, he visited Anna Joy before spending his last few hours saying goodbye to his girlfriend.

"I want you to know how much I love you. If you weren't my cousin, I'd marry you. But you are so innocent, and you need to know that men are no good. We have one thing on our minds. You can't trust us. You need to know this before I go because I may not come back." He hugged her tight, kissed her on the cheek, and departed.

Three months later, he shipped out to Vietnam, only to come back in a few months encased in a flag-draped box.

·｡ৎ৶ঌ｡·

Anna Joy curled up in a chair in the office of Sister Alphonsus—her teacher and her best friend at the college—sobs mingling with quiet screams. As she pounded the desk, her untouched soup splashed over its rim. The image of the two marines standing at attention on the front stoop of her aunt and uncle's home was etched in her mind. Her beloved cousin Jimmy, her champion, had been killed in Vietnam.

She huddled in the office, too numb to go to class, but not anesthetized enough to block the pangs of loss squeezing her chest. Hugging the box of tissues, she rocked back and forth until one by one she crumpled them in the trash.

The words from class lectures had floated about her, incomprehensible, blotted out by waves of grief. Her lifeblood gauge teetered on empty.

14.

Screwy Louie

I will never leave you nor forsake you.

Hebrews 13:5 (NKJV)

Anna Joy gnawed on her lower lip. Her hands trembled as she dialed the phone. "Auntie? Can you take me to the hospital?"

"What's the matter? Are you sick?"

"I feel like I'm going crazy. I just can't take it anymore." A sob escaped her lips. "I want you to take me to the psychiatric unit." Anna Joy twisted the phone cord in her hand. "You know I can't ask Mom. She wouldn't understand." Her mom thought shrinks were quacks.

"I'll be right over."

"Thanks." Anna Joy cradled the phone and breathed a sigh of relief. She stared at her packed bag. She knew Auntie would help. She was hurting too, ever since her son Jimmy had died in Vietnam.

Auntie strode into the apartment and grabbed Anna Joy's suitcase. "Let's go." They rode in silence to the emergency room entrance. Auntie deposited Anna Joy's bag at the check-in desk. "Call me when you're ready to come home."

Anna Joy stared at Auntie's retreating form, drew in a deep breath, and turned toward the woman seated at the desk.

"How can I help you?" The woman repeated her question, peering at Anna Joy over her spectacles.

Anna Joy glanced down at her lap. "I need to see a psychiatrist."

After gathering Anna Joy's information, the woman directed her to a chair in the waiting room. "Someone will be with you shortly."

She heard her name called and glanced up at a woman, clad in all white, standing in the doorway. A starched cap perched atop her updo. Anna Joy pulled herself up with her crutches. "My suitcase is over there."

The nurse clasped a metal chart in one hand and, with the other, retrieved the suitcase. "Follow me." She led Anna Joy into a cubicle separated from other patients only by a pale curtain and helped her onto the cart. "The doctor will be in shortly."

.✿✿✿.

The curtain hooks rattled and startled Anna Joy.

A man, graying at the temples and wearing a white coat, stepped into her cubicle and introduced himself. He sat down on the nearby stool and opened her chart. "How can we help you today?"

"I feel like I'm going crazy. I can't sleep. I can't go to class . . ." Her voice trailed off. She felt like she couldn't breathe, suffocated by the waves of pain crashing over her.

Ever since Jimmy, her favorite cousin and champion, had died in Vietnam a few months earlier, she had skipped classes. She never told her mother. Her favorite college teacher, Sister Alphonsus, allowed Anna Joy to sit in her office and cry during class time. Sister Alphonsus also negotiated an incomplete for the semester and arranged for Anna Joy to make up her classes in summer school.

"I just can't go on." Anna Joy looked down at her quivering hands. She couldn't stop shaking.

The doctor admitted her to the psychiatric unit under the care of Dr. Louis.

Anna Joy walked into the dining room on the mental health ward and sat down at a table near the door. One by one, a few other women sat down at her table. Finally, one of the women looked up from her plastic tray. "You new here?"

She nodded. "I'm Anna Joy."

"Which doctor did you get assigned to?" the woman asked between bites, waving her plastic fork.

"Doctor Louis."

The woman laughed and shook her head. "Ah! They stuck you with Screwy Louie!"

"Screwy Louie?"

"You'll find out." The woman got up from the table, grabbed her tray, and walked out.

What did she mean? Anna Joy glanced at the other women seated at her table, hunched over their trays. Silence.

The next morning, Anna Joy asked a nurse for directions to the group therapy room. The hollow tap of her rubber-tipped crutches echoed through the corridor. She peeked into the room, slipped in, and sat down in the nearest empty chair. She stole a glance around the circle of fellow attendees. A few laughed and joked; others stared at the floor in silence.

A small-boned man seated across from Anna Joy repeatedly pushed his gray hair off his forehead. His attempts didn't seem to make much difference since shocks of hair poked out of his head in all directions. He peered at her through his thick horn-rimmed spectacles, perched askew across his beaked nose. He crossed one leg over the other, adjusted the tails of his white coat, and cleared his throat. "For those of you who don't know me, I'm Dr. Louis, a staff psychiatrist."

Anna Joy listened to the others, not sure how these group sessions would be of any help to her. How could these people understand her grief?

.⁓ֶ୭ℓﻉכ.

The nurses encouraged patients to spend time in group activities, whether music, art, or games—as long as the game pieces were too large to swallow. Anna Joy joined a few other patients in the craft room.

The art therapist tore off large sheets of white paper from a roll and placed a sheet in front of each person. She laid a smock and a palette of non-toxic paints at each place setting. "Today, we are going to fingerpaint. Finger painting is a great way to express ourselves, to get in touch with our feelings and our emotions."

"I feel like I'm back in kindergarten," the woman next to Anna Joy grumbled. "Yesterday, I wanted to cut a piece of paper, and I had to ask someone to cut it for me. They wouldn't even let me use the scissors."

Anna Joy slipped the paint-stained smock over her clothes, relieved that even her uncoordinated fingers could streak paint across the sheet. She dipped her finger into the green paint and swirled her favorite color across the paper.

.⁓ֶ୭ℓﻉכ.

Anna Joy settled into the routine of the psychiatric ward, wandering from one scheduled activity to the next. She felt safe. She listened to other patients share their therapy experiences and how their doctors were helping them. But not so for the patients of Dr. Louis. His patients seemed to receive more help from one another. If not for his white coat, it would be difficult to distinguish him from one of the patients. Hence his nickname—Screwy Louie.

Anna Joy walked into Dr. Louis's office once again for her scheduled one-on-one appointment time. She lowered herself into a chair across from him and anticipated enduring another wasted hour. File folders littered his desk except for one corner where a pipe rested in an ashtray. Bookcases filled with a haphazard array of medical books covered one wall. Psychiatric journals lay strewn in piles across the floor. She wondered if he ever read them.

He shuffled through the papers on his desk until he finally found the file he wanted and opened the folder. "How are you today, Anna Joy?" He lit his pipe and sat back in his chair. A curl of smoke with a sweet, woodsy aroma drifted toward her.

She squirmed. "I'm doing about the same." No matter what she said, nothing the doctor could say or do would bring Jimmy back or stop the pain bursting in her chest.

"You've been here several weeks now. You seem calmer than when you first arrived and have been doing well with all your therapy. I'm not sure there is anything more we can do for you here." He puffed his pipe and leaned forward. "There's only one thing wrong with you, Anna Joy."

Anna Joy looked up, her gaze locked onto Doctor Louis's piercing blue eyes. Did she detect caring in his tone?

"You need someone who can love you twenty-four seven." He pursed his lips. "Unfortunately, there is no such person."

.ᘇ୧ᘆ.

Screwy Louie got one thing right. She needed someone to love her twenty-four seven. But one thing he got wrong—there was such a person. Anna Joy found her twenty-four-seven love when she encountered Jesus.

15.

A Spiritual Father

For even if you had ten thousand others to teach you about Christ, you have only one spiritual father. For I became your father in Christ Jesus when I preached the Good News to you.

1 Corinthians 4:15 (NLT)

"Lord, if you don't want me to take my life, you're going to have to give me the power to resist." Anna Joy clamped her hands around her head. "These voices are too strong for me!"

She had checked in to a cheap motel. No one knew where she was. No one would find her until morning. She flipped open the bottle of pills, downed the tablets, and curled up on the bed. She waited. Soon the pills would swallow her pain.

"Get up!"

A voice broke through her fuzziness. Was she dreaming?

"Get up!" The voice said again. "Go into the bathroom and throw up those pills."

Anna Joy stumbled into the bathroom and vomited the pills. "Nothing has changed. I can't live like this," she said. "Who are you?"

"I am Jesus," the voice said and laid his hands on her head. "And I brought the power."

Instantly, the fog of grogginess lifted as if she had never popped the pills. Wide-awake, Anna Joy scanned the room, searching for the source of the voice that rescued her from death.

.ᴕᏜᧉᴕ.

Ever since she had tried to end her life, Anna Joy felt a tug-of-war in her spirit. She felt pulled toward witchcraft, hearing voices in her head screaming their threats, attempting to drown out the Holy Spirit.

"Please don't go in there," a voice whispered.

She tightened her grip on the crutches, deliberately striking the pavement. With each step, she stomped toward the witchcraft coven, despite the plea from the Holy Spirit.

"You don't belong here," she said to the Holy Spirit.

"Neither do you," the voice whispered. "But if you go, I go. I won't leave you."

She cried out, "I'm so confused!"

What had happened that night when Jesus thwarted her suicide attempt? "I need some answers," she said. "I'll talk to a priest."

.ᴕᏜᧉᴕ.

"I don't know what happened to you," the priest said later when she met with him. "You are either very close to heaven or very close to hell. I don't know."

She visited priest after priest in the city and received similar responses.

Refusing to give up, Anna Joy opted to reach out one more time. One of her favorite college teachers was a priest, Father Andrew, who had been recently reassigned out of state. She pulled out her stationery and began writing a four-line note. Several hours later she scrawled the last lines of a nine-page, tear-slashed letter. "I hate the English language. It doesn't have enough words. Please come! And hurry!"

"I have not experienced the Holy Spirit in the way you describe," Father Andrew wrote. "But hang on! I'm coming, and I'll bring someone who can tell you what happened to you."

.·~⊶⊷~·.

Father Andrew arrived to participate in an event sponsored by Anna Joy's college called The Pentecostal Movement in the Catholic Church. He accompanied David, one of his students, who would be speaking.

Anna Joy walked into the church, her heart racing. Maybe today she would get some answers. She also looked forward to seeing her old friend, Father Andrew.

Father Andrew drew her into a hug, then turned toward David. "Let me introduce you."

"I know her," David said.

"How do you know me? We've never met."

"You don't want to know that now." He wrapped his arms around her. They felt like the same arms that comforted her the night Jesus came into the room and brought the power.

"Jesus?" she whispered.

"Yes. He sent me."

Anna Joy leaned forward, trying to catch every word of David's talk.

Afterward, David sat down with her, a thick, dog-eared Bible on his lap. He flipped through his Bible, explaining the Scriptures and the infilling of the Holy Spirit. "You wondered how I knew you. The Lord showed me a picture of you in a dream and even told me your name. He's the reason I boarded the plane. He's the reason I came to see you."

After David shared all that was on his heart and prayed for her, he said, "Do you have a Bible?"

She shook her head.

"Here, take mine."

The next day, he boarded a plane for home. But now he had a new baby in the Spirit to care for and teach her how to grow in the knowledge of the Lord.

David sent Anna Joy three letters a week, eighteen pages double-sided, filled with whole passages of Scripture. He knew she wasn't reading the Bible. But he knew she would read his letters, and David's letters became her path to the Bible.

After three years of devouring his letters, Anna Joy had an idea. "I can write Bible passages to David too." She opened her Bible and searched for passages to send him. It seemed like the verses jumped off the page. She grinned as she jotted them down. "Did you know the Bible says this?" She could hardly contain her excitement as she poured out her newfound Scripture verses in her letters.

David's letters changed. During the next year, he no longer wrote out the passages of Scripture but only the reference.

"You don't need David anymore," the Lord would eventually say after four years of letters and phone conversations. "I'm going to take him away. You have two ways in which you can let him go. You can let go with open hands, and he'll always be your friend and take care of you. But if you close your fist and hang on to him, you'll never see him again."

Anna Joy relinquished holding on to her special friend who had been to her what Paul had been to many believers—a spiritual father.

16.

Sister Gladys

*Allow the healing words you've heard from me to live
in you and make them a model for life as your faith
and love for the Anointed One grows even more.*

2 Timothy 1:13 (TPT)

"I have someone I want you to meet." David grinned and placed his hand on Anna Joy's arm. The line of people waiting for prayer from the woman standing at the front of the church had dwindled. She spotted David and Anna Joy. Her floor-length dress swept over the carpet and stirred the fragrance of her heavy perfume as she approached them. Her voluminous updo enhanced her commanding presence.

Anna Joy leaned against the wooden pew and extended her hand, anticipating a handshake or a hello.

Instead, the woman slapped her hand on Anna Joy's forehead and said, "Spirit of fear, come out of her!"

Anna Joy fell backward on the floor.

David reached out to catch her, but she slipped past him. He assisted her as she struggled to her feet.

Anna Joy straightened her dress, raised her eyebrows, and stared at the woman standing in front of her. "Do you always greet people this way?"

"There was none of you to greet. The spirit of fear was so strong that I couldn't find you. And I don't talk to spirits." She smiled. "I'm Sister Gladys."

"Anna Joy. I just moved here."

David had promised to introduce her to people who could help her if she would relocate. Despite all the Scripture and love David had poured into her for the past few years, she knew she needed more help. She longed for freedom from the voices that tormented her and spewed lies and accusations.

"Sister Gladys, this is the woman I was telling you about. I was hoping you could help her find a job and a place to live," David said.

Sister Gladys turned toward Anna Joy. "What type of work have you done?"

"I worked as a telephone operator." She had enjoyed her job, especially the split shifts that no one else wanted to take. Even though she sensed the Lord leading her to quit the job and relocate, she wrestled with the decision. She would be leaving her mom and the two-room apartment they shared, her coworkers, and the people in her church fellowship who faithfully drove across town to give her rides to church and Bible study. Besides, her handicap hampered employment opportunities. No one wanted to hire a girl with a disability despite her college education.

She recalled the day when she finally turned in her resignation. Her supervisor had said, "I'm glad you decided to resign; otherwise I would have to fire you. It's not that you don't do good work, but you need too many bathroom breaks. Takes you away from the switchboard too often and for too long."

Anna Joy hung her head, cheeks burning. She couldn't help it. Her bladder spasmed, and she needed frequent restroom trips to avoid the humiliation of accidents. But the Lord's timing had been perfect. He had known she would be terminated from her job.

Sister Gladys paused and furrowed her brow. "Hmm. I might have a place for you to live. Maybe you can help out with light household tasks for a disabled couple until you find a job."

Anna Joy nodded.

A little boy charged up the aisle and wrapped his arms around Sister Gladys's waist. His eyes shone as he gazed into her smiling face and signed, "I love you."

She signed back, "I love you, and Jesus loves you too."

As the boy ran off, she turned to Anna Joy and smiled. "Children recognize the Spirit of God in you even if they don't understand why they're attracted to you."

Many children flocked to Sister Gladys over the years. No matter how tired she was or how much her feet ached from hours of standing and ministering, she grinned and hugged each one.

.⸲ᘻᓬᖇ.

Sister Gladys loved to teach about the Old Testament tabernacle, spiritual warfare, and the cross. Many days she arrived at the church with dark circles under her eyes, having either prayed through the night for a troubled soul or ministered to someone in a crisis.

She took Anna Joy under her wing. She recognized the giftings and callings God had placed within this woman. Anna Joy may have been physically disabled, but she was spiritually gifted. Gifts of discernment, intercession, and counsel.

With Anna Joy in tow, Sister Gladys assembled her prayer teams for ministry. In the middle of a session, she would turn to her and say, "What are you discerning here?"

At first Anna Joy hesitated, unsure if what she sensed was correct. What if she was wrong? She glanced down. Her cheeks flushed when she sensed Sister Gladys's eyes still fixed on her, waiting. Finally, Anna Joy mumbled what she sensed God saying.

Sister Gladys smiled. "That's correct."

.⸲ᘻᓬᖇ.

Over time, Anna Joy's confidence grew as she realized she could hear God's voice too. For eight years, she ministered on prayer teams under Sister Gladys's tutelage, growing in her relationship with the Lord and in wisdom, counsel, and discernment. She also experienced God's healing and freedom from the tormenting voices.

Many years later, Anna Joy would smile and say, "Sister Gladys taught me how to survive. Because of her, I'm alive today."

17.

Ruby

Serve wholeheartedly, as if you were serving the Lord, not people.

Ephesians 6:7 (NIV)

David grabbed Anna Joy's bags out of the trunk of his car and carried them up to the front porch of the small ranch-style home. He turned, waited for her to catch up, and then knocked on the door. Yapping dogs responded.

Anna Joy leaned on her crutches. It seemed to take a long time for someone to come to the door. Was anyone home? Sister Gladys said she had called and made arrangements for her to stay with this couple and help out until she could find a job.

Finally, the door opened, and Anna Joy looked down into the wrinkly face of a gray-haired woman leaning on her petite wooden crutches.

The woman pulled herself up to her not-quite-four-foot-tall height, including the bun on top of her head. "You must be Anna Joy. I'm Ruby. Come on in." She stepped aside, and with her shortened arm, she beckoned them in. "Over there is my husband, Frank." She pointed her crutch toward a man whose six-foot frame extended over the footrest of an overstuffed recliner. His head hung over to one side, his ear nearly touching his shoulder. He mumbled a few words that sounded more like inaudible grunts. Drool slipped out the side of his mouth and streamed down his chin.

"And that's Peter." A disheveled young man seated next to Frank turned his head toward Anna Joy, gave a slight nod, and turned back to the television screen. "He comes over and helps take care of Frank. I don't know if Sister Gladys told you, but Frank has Parkinson's."

Anna Joy and David stepped into the living room. Noxious odors of pets and waste rankled her nostrils. Even the floral pattern on the sagging sofa couldn't camouflage the tufts of dog fur.

Ruby directed them toward a room in the back.

Anna Joy and David navigated past the dogs, clutter, and filth to the bedroom. The room seemed cleaner and tidier than the rest of the house.

Ruby trailed behind. "It's a nice room. You should be comfortable here. I cleared the closet and dresser for you." She turned around, headed back to the living room, and hoisted herself onto the sofa with the assistance of her crutches. Her legs extended over the edge of the cushion but were too short to dangle.

David deposited Anna Joy's suitcases on the bed, bent down, and whispered. "Are you going to be okay here?"

She gulped and looked up at him with doe eyes, "You can go if you need to."

He hugged her. "You have my number. Let me know if you need anything. I mean anything."

Anna Joy nodded. She wouldn't be bothering David. He was headed back to college. She glanced around the room and sighed, "I guess I'd better unpack. I have my work cut out for me."

.ₒ୬ℰ୬.

Anna Joy gathered the laundry. On her hands and knees, she pushed the pile into the laundry room, grateful she had scrubbed the grime off the floors first. She grasped the edge of the washer, pulled herself up, lifted the lid, and drew back. A new stench assaulted her. She thought she had rid the house of most of the non-recurring foul odors and filth. Her reddened hands testified to all her scrubbing. She pulled out the washer filter enmeshed with green-black gunk. The laundry would have to wait. Hanging over the wash basin, she grabbed a brush and scrubbed the filter until sweat beaded on her forehead.

Finally, she could start the laundry. She wished Peter would at least rinse or pretreat Frank's clothing—caked with food that had dribbled out of his mouth when Peter fed him—and Frank's soiled bedding. At least Peter faithfully came and helped dress and feed Frank. Occasionally Anna Joy fed Frank, a painstakingly slow process since he struggled to swallow. But he rewarded her efforts with the gratitude reflected in his eyes.

.·୭ℓℯ౦.

Between going to church meetings with Sister Gladys, Anna Joy cleaned, cooked, and shopped. Since Ruby rarely left home, Anna Joy wondered why others in the church didn't come to visit or offer to help. But she soon gleaned from Ruby that most people could not handle all her dogs or the odors. The dogs had free rein of the house, and dust and dog hair blanketed every seating area. "My dogs are the only company 1 have. Maybe if people came and visited, I wouldn't need my dogs."

Ruby bred Pomeranians. Sometimes she acquired so many that she placed a bed for an expectant dog in every room. Her reputation preceded her as the best dog midwife. When people anticipated birthing problems with their precious Poms, they brought them to Ruby.

"Anna Joy, Anna Joy!" Ruby called out one night. "Get up!"

Anna Joy stirred and glanced at the clock. *It's the middle of the night.* "Ruby, what's wrong?"

"Get in here and help me. Precious is in labor and having a hard time. There's only one pup, and it's too big. I don't intend to lose either one. I don't know why people don't consider the size of the stud when breeding. He was too big, and I warned the owner she could have trouble if there was only one puppy, especially if it was a big puppy. But she wouldn't listen." Ruby huffed as she walked back into the living room.

Anna Joy wound her way around the other dog beds to Ruby. Precious seemed lethargic. Anna Joy lowered herself down at the dog's head.

"I want you to hold on to Precious and keep her calm. I have to get inside and pull the pup out." Ruby squirted lubricant on her gloved hands, reached in, and grabbed hold of the puppy. She firmly but gently extracted her from the birth canal.

Precious whimpered and squirmed beneath Anna Joy's hands.

"Is the puppy okay?" Anna Joy watched Ruby clear the puppy's nose and mouth with a tiny bulb syringe and then vigorously rub her with a towel. Finally, she heard a high-pitched squeak. Anna Joy let out the deep breath she was unaware she had been holding.

Ruby laid the puppy next to Precious. Precious turned her head and licked her rooting puppy.

"You can go back to bed now. I can handle it from here," Ruby said.

18.

Groceries

And my God shall supply all your need according
to His riches in glory by Christ Jesus.

Philippians 4:19 (NKJV)

Anna Joy's stomach growled. She opened the cupboard and scanned the shelves for breakfast food. A nearly empty box of cereal and several cans of food lay strewn across the bare shelves. She checked the refrigerator. A few condiments, a little juice, and a bit of milk. What was that smell? She bent down and reached her hand into the back of the refrigerator. She extracted something green and unidentifiable. Holding the offending object between her fingertips, she scrunched her face and dropped the unopened container into the waste basket.

Ruby perched on her crutches in the doorway. "I guess we need some groceries. Make a list of what we need." She turned and walked away.

Anna Joy sat down at the table and started her list. The list grew longer and longer as she planned how to fill the cupboards and refrigerator with enough food to feed four, including Peter, since he ate most of his meals with Frank. She smiled as she scanned her list. This should do. She even included two kinds of cheese, Ruby's favorite and hers. At the end of the list, she scrawled *Hershey's bars with almonds*, her favorite chocolate.

"I made our list!" Anna Joy waved the paper at Ruby, who had appeared in the doorway. "How do you want me to pay for them?"

"There is no money." Ruby turned and paused before walking away. "You know how to pray, don't you?" She didn't wait for an answer. "Pray for the groceries we need. And don't forget doggie treats."

Anna Joy's mouth hung open as she stared at Ruby's retreating form. Pray? For groceries? She slid onto the kitchen chair and clasped her head in her hands. *Oh, Lord, help!*

She examined her list. Maybe she needed to cut out some of the items. I guess we don't need two kinds of cheese. She hesitated, then crossed off her favorite, leaving Ruby's choice. She crossed out the Hershey's bars. They were a luxury.

Head bowed, hands trembling, Anna Joy could almost hear her heart pound as she prayed. "Lord, you know what we need. You know I can't make any meals with what we have on hand. We have no money. You said you would supply what we need, so I lift this list to you and ask you to provide for us. Thank you, Lord."

She had no sooner finished praying when the doorbell rang. Ruby wasn't in sight, so Anna Joy navigated around the barking dogs and opened the door.

A man dressed in a white store delivery uniform stood in the doorway holding brown paper bags overflowing with groceries. "Where would you like me to put these bags?"

"I think you have the wrong house. We didn't order anything."

"This is your address, right?" He recited the address and smiled. "So, I'm at the right place. Should I put these in the kitchen?"

Dumbfounded, Anna Joy nodded, stepped back, and motioned toward the kitchen.

After carrying in the six bags of groceries, the man nodded. "Have a blessed day!" He walked to his truck and drove away.

Anna Joy blinked. Did he actually drive away? The truck just seemed to—disappear.

She riffled through the groceries, filling the shelves and stocking the refrigerator. Everything she had on her list was accounted for, including two kinds of cheese and the Hershey's almond bars. *Thank you, Lord! You did it! You answered my prayer!*

Anna Joy had written down the name of the store painted on the side of the white truck, but when she checked the phone book, she couldn't find the name of the supermarket listed. She had never heard of that chain before. Maybe it was a local market.

Ruby grinned from ear to ear. "The Lord heard our prayers and has taken care of us once again."

"Where is this store located?"

"Never heard of it." Ruby's Pomeranian confronted her, begging for a treat. She dug around in her pocket, pulled out a doggie treat, and held it out for her precious canine. "Are you sure you got the store's name right?"

Later, Anna Joy asked others if they had heard of the grocery store that delivered those six bags of groceries. No one had.

19.

Lesson on a Dime

To the faithful you show yourself faithful.

Psalm 18:25 (NLT)

Anna Joy surveyed the hotel ballroom, hoping to find someone she recognized. She had never been in such a fancy room with velvet curtains and crystal chandeliers. Sister Gladys must be here somewhere. But she would probably be on the platform. Anna Joy slipped into a seat in the back, on the aisle and close to a restroom. She looked forward to her first regional Christian conference. The room buzzed with anticipation as each seat filled. Strains of familiar hymns and choruses soon permeated the room. The voices and instruments seemed to hint at the sounds of heaven.

When it was time for the offering. Anna Joy didn't need to check her coin purse. She knew she only had ten dimes. Surely God didn't want her coins.

"I want my tithe," she sensed the Lord whisper.

Did God really say that? It was just ten cents.

"I want my tithe."

Anna Joy slid open the zipper of her coin purse. If she gave away her dime, she wouldn't have enough money for a sandwich and Coke at lunchtime. She slipped the dime into the bucket as it passed. Oh well, she would participate in one of the first lessons Sister Gladys had taught her—fasting. Sister Gladys frequently expounded on the importance of fasting for ministry.

At lunch break, the crowd clambered out of their chairs and exited the ballroom. Anna Joy waited until the room emptied before heading to the restroom. She walked too slowly for the crowd and didn't want to get tripped by someone. The plush carpet muffled the tap of her crutches as she joined the end of the restroom line. She waited her turn, half-listening to the chatter of the other women. As she rounded the corner, her eyes widened. An attendant distributed cloth towels in the brocaded room with ornate wash bowls. She didn't know such a fancy place existed.

Since she didn't have enough money for lunch and nowhere to go, Anna Joy returned to the ballroom after exiting the restroom. She could read her Bible while she waited for the afternoon session to start.

"Excuse me." A man's voice interrupted her reading.

She looked up.

"I have an extra sandwich and Coke. Would you like to have it?"

Anna Joy grinned. "Thank you!"

The man handed her the sandwich and Coke and walked away.

"You did it, Lord! You did it for me! Sister Gladys said we could never out-give God. I got lunch and ninety cents too." She enjoyed her lunch, but even more so, relished God's faithfulness.

Sister Gladys strode by her on her way to the platform. She stopped in front of Anna Joy. "When the meeting is over tonight, don't leave. Wait. The Holy Spirit shows up when unbelief leaves."

After the evening meeting, the people around her gathered their belongings and hurried out. A few remained seated, scattered throughout the ballroom. A hush filled the room. Waiting. Praying.

Soft strains of "alleluia, alleluia" broke out.

Anna Joy sat and waited, watching those around her, those more spiritually mature like Sister Gladys. Some were on their faces. Others kneeling.

Sobs erupted from one corner and cries from another as the presence of the Holy Spirit filled the room. From deep within, she felt an intense joy bubbling up. "Jesus!" Thankfully she was sitting down because her legs probably wouldn't hold her upright. She felt as though her flesh would burst open if the Lord's presence grew any stronger.

Sometime after midnight, the leaders packed up. The visitation of the Holy Spirit was over. At least, for now.

20.

Dusted off Memories
and a Dust Storm

Hear, O LORD, and have mercy on me; LORD, be my helper!"

Psalm 30:10 (NKJV)

"We grew up in bayou country." Ruby chuckled and shook her head. She opened her mouth as if to speak, but instead of continuing to tell Anna Joy about her childhood, her gaze darted toward the window. She furrowed her brow and hopped off the couch. "Hurry! Close the windows. Make sure the doors are shut tight."

The living room had suddenly darkened. Ruby hobbled past Peter to the back door. "You too, Peter!" She called the dogs in, bribing them with treats, slammed the doggie door shut, and locked it.

Anna Joy headed to the nearest window and slammed it shut. A dark cloud hovered in the distance. "I don't remember anyone saying we were getting storms."

"That's not rain. That cloud is a sandstorm heading right toward us." Ruby puffed as she hustled from window to window, making sure they were sealed tightly.

The wind swirled around the house, churning the sandy soil. Anna Joy's eyes widened as the windowpane clouded over, reducing visibility.

The storm disappeared as fast as it arrived, leaving a residue of grit on the windowsills and in the doorways. Anna Joy coughed, choking on the fine granules. Her sinuses immediately felt congested.

"Get the vacuum and mop. We'll have to vacuum the upholstery too!" Ruby grabbed a bucket and some rags and attacked the windowsills.

Anna Joy pulled out the mop, vacuum, and all the attachments. They moved from room to room with cleaning products in tow. No matter how much she mopped, vacuumed, and scoured, stray dust particles danced a tormenting jig throughout the house. *Please help me, Lord.* If this was the kind of storm the Southwest experienced, no wonder the house never seemed clean.

Ruby hoisted herself onto the couch and exhaled through puffed cheeks. She peered at Anna Joy. Sweat had mingled with the dust and streaked their faces. "I need to rest a spell before we strip the beds."

Anna Joy sighed as she plopped next to her. Maybe a little conversation would provide a distraction from this awful mess. "You were telling me about your childhood, Ruby."

"Oh yes! There were eleven of us. Every other one of us kids was born with dwarfism. Not all my brothers and sisters survived to adulthood. My parents had no clue what caused us to be born this way since neither of them was a little person. At that time, the doctors didn't know that dwarfism is genetic.

"We just thought we were normal kids growing up in alligator country. One day I was walking home from school, and an alligator poked his snout through the reeds. He snapped at me, and then he chased me! I was so scared. I started running on my short legs with my crutches as fast as I could, screaming, 'Daddy, Daddy, get your gun!' He grabbed his gun from over the doorway and shot at the alligator before that old gator snatched me." Ruby laughed.

After a while, Ruby slipped off the couch. "We better get those beds stripped."

Anna Joy followed. Her muscles ached in protest. It seemed like she had just washed all the bedding. But she was grateful for Ruby's help. Most of the housekeeping duties had fallen upon Anna Joy since her arrival. In the meantime, she hoped Peter would wipe down the high cabinets and windows she couldn't reach. Maybe Ruby would tell her more about her childhood on another day.

21.

Healings and Heartbreaks

Heal me, O LORD, and I shall be healed; Save me,
and I shall be saved, For You are my praise.

Jeremiah 17:14 (NKJV)

Some sang hymns, others prayed as they crowded near the entrance of the auditorium, waiting for the doors to open. Maybe today was her day for a miracle.

Anna Joy leaned against the wall and shifted her weight from one foot to the other. She had been standing for several hours, and her leg muscles spasmed and cramped again. If she left, she'd never get her place back in line. Besides, dozens of wheelchairs propping up the young and old had boxed her in. She craned her neck to peer around the corner, but she could no longer see the end of the line. Or what was once a line. A throng of people hungry for a touch from God wound around the building.

Anna Joy swiped the beads of perspiration from her brow once again. Steam seemed to rise from the pavement, trapped by the sweaty bodies surrounding her. The odor rankled her nostrils.

The doors opened. She grabbed her crutches and squeezed through the door with the crowd, hoping no one would cause her to trip. She hurried to the front row and sat down, glancing at the boy in a wheelchair parked next to her. She quickly averted her gaze and shuddered. Scars from third-degree burns covered his body and deformed his face. She stole a glance at the person who flanked her other side. A child sat lopsided in a stroller-type wheelchair. Contractures had curled his extremities.

Her stomach rumbled, reminding her she hadn't had anything to eat or drink since she left home. Anna Joy licked her parched lips. Even though the meeting could last six hours, she didn't dare vacate her seat. People scurried up and down the aisles, scanning the rows, ready to pounce on any vacant chair.

The atmosphere seemed charged with electricity as the crowds waited for the woman to appear on stage. Their voices faded into reverence when strains from her theme song drifted throughout the auditorium. The woman, in a flowing floor-length dress, glided onto the platform.

"I believe in miracles. Because I believe in God."

With her lilting voice, the woman shared about Jesus and the person of the Holy Spirit. With help from the choir, she led the congregation in worship. Choruses of "He Touched Me" and "Alleluia" filled the auditorium.

At one point, the atmosphere seemed to shift. She called out various diseases and maladies she sensed the Lord healing. "When you know God has healed you, come up to the platform and testify to what the Lord has done for you."

People from all over the auditorium left their seats, walked, and even ran to the platform. A few pushed empty wheelchairs into the throng.

As Anna Joy prayed, she looked to her right and to her left. All down her row, each person on either side of her experienced healing. Some hopped out of wheelchairs and raced to the platform to share their miracle. She watched, mesmerized, as the child's contractures straightened. She glanced at the other boy next to her and stared. Was he the same boy with the third-degree burns? His skin was as smooth as a newborn baby's. She glanced down at her legs, dangling over the edge of the chair. Maybe if she tried to stand . . .

But as her feet touched the floor, nothing had changed. Her lower lip trembled as tears slid down her cheeks. She sat down and stared at her crutches lying on the floor.

Before long, Anna Joy spotted the hem of a flowing dress swishing in front of her. She raised her gaze. The lady stood in front of her for what seemed like forever. Love and compassion spilled from her eyes. The woman furrowed her brow and shook her head. "Not yet, honey." She turned and walked back up onto the platform.

Several weeks later, Anna Joy received a letter from this woman, who believed in miracles. *How did she get my address?* She hadn't told the lady her name. Yet this woman took the time to write to her. With trembling hands, Anna Joy opened the envelope and slipped out the single sheet of paper. She read and reread the words written by the woman who prayed for thousands of people each month. She clutched the paper to her chest and sobbed. *Lord, she promised to pray for me. You didn't forget me!*

22.

Gert and Harry

A longing fulfilled is sweet to the soul.

Proverbs 13:19 (NIV)

Gert held the door of her ranch-style home for Anna Joy and called over her shoulder, "Girls! I have someone I want you to meet." She turned back to Anna Joy. "They're probably still cleaning."

As each of the three girls peeked around the corners of various rooms, Gert introduced her daughters. "Anna Joy's my prayer partner and the newest member of our prayer team." Gert beamed with pride as she wrapped her arm around Anna Joy's shoulder and pulled her into a hug.

Anna Joy blushed as she greeted each girl. She glanced around the living room. Not a speck of dust. Not a knick-knack out of place.

"Let's get some lunch." Gert led the way into the kitchen and pulled out a chair for Anna Joy.

Gert's daughter Lisa returned to her task of washing used bread bags. She opened each one and stood it upright in the dish drainer.

Gert bustled around the kitchen. She pulled out various sandwich fixings from plastic bread bags and set them on the table. "Did you take the waxed paper out of the cereal boxes?"

Lisa nodded and pointed to the pile of neatly folded waxed paper in the corner of the counter.

"Harry insists we reuse everything: waxed paper in cereal boxes, bread bags, brown paper bags, and whatever else he happens to think of." Gert shook her head.

"We used to put bread bags over our shoes in the winter before we put on our boots to keep our feet dry." Anna Joy remembered Auntie scrounging in the drawer for bags before school while chiding the boys for their carelessness that had ripped the previous day's bags.

Another daughter carried a laundry basket overflowing with plush towels through the kitchen on her way to the laundry room.

"Wow! That's a lot of towels." Anna Joy took another bite from her sandwich. A sandwich had never tasted so good. Maybe it was because someone else made it for her.

"Well, there's five of us. That's two towels and two washcloths apiece every couple of days."

Anna Joy gulped. At Auntie's house, thin, ragged towels hung haphazardly from two towel bars. When they bathed, the kids often shared one towel and one washcloth. Auntie only washed once a week unless there was a baby.

"Cleanliness is next to godliness." Gert shrugged her shoulders and dug into her sandwich.

A man in gray coveralls trudged into the kitchen. "What's for lunch?"

Gert got up from the table. "Harry, this is Anna Joy." She opened the refrigerator and, once again, pulled out the sandwich fixings.

Harry nodded. "Hello." He turned back to Gert, took the plate she handed to him, and returned to his workroom.

"I'll have to do the books for the business later. He's had a lot of plumbing calls lately."

"Knock, knock." Anna Joy rapped her knuckles on the doorframe of Harry's workroom. "Can I come in?"

Harry glanced up from tinkering with his fixtures. Various tools lay strewn across his wooden workbench. He peered at her over his glasses. "I guess so. Not much to see," he mumbled as he pulled up a chair for Anna Joy. He returned to his stool and examined his work. "Gert and the girls never come back here unless they have to." He hunched over his project. "Too messy and dirty, I guess."

Anna Joy scanned the room filled with tools, electronics, and various gadgets haphazardly arrayed on shelves, tables, and the floor. She sat down. "What are you working on?"

"I'm trying to find the right fitting to seal a bathtub leak in an old house. They just don't make parts like they used to." He reached for another metal part and tried to piece together a working fixture.

Anna Joy possessed zero knowledge of plumbing and electronics. "How does it work?"

Harry looked at her with raised eyebrows and shook his head. "I'm not used to anyone asking me how things work." He held up the apparatus and explained an abridged version of his project.

·ᴈᴥᴇ·

Thereafter, whenever Anna Joy visited Gert, she would stop by Harry's workshop, if he was in, and chat. Often she didn't understand what Harry explained, but she knew if Gert was her friend, she needed to befriend Harry too. Through the years, she had learned the art of making friends by asking open-ended questions about their interests, even if she had no personal interest in their passions.

At first, Harry had offered short answers to her questions, but one day, when Anna Joy showed up at his workroom door, his face brightened. "Come in! How are you today, Anna Joy?" He pulled out the special chair he had brought into his workroom just for her.

"I'm fine. What are you working on today?"

"I'm trying to get this radio to work again." He shook his head.

"I don't understand how they can call today's music, music. The girls want one of those new-fangled stereo systems. I can't see buying them one when they have a perfectly good record player. This radio will work just fine when I get it fixed."

"Have you checked out the new stereo systems?" Even though each of his girls had begged her to talk to their dad about getting them a new stereo system, Anna Joy knew, as far as Harry was concerned, if something worked it was good enough. But she understood the girls' desire. She'd love to have a stereo component system with earphones. She would curl up on her bed with a cat, put on the earphones, and block out the TV and the barking dogs. Maybe someday, she'd be able to tuck away enough money to buy one. She knew she could never afford a top-of-the-line system like the one her dad had given to her half sister, Janet. But she could dream.

"These new systems are really nice. Great sound. They advertise them in my electronics magazine." He riffled through a stack of magazines and catalogs until he found the one he wanted, flipped to the designated page, and handed the issue to Anna Joy.

"Wow! They're amazing. When I save up enough money, will you help me pick one out?" Of course, at this rate, it may take years to save enough money, but no matter. She wouldn't think about that.

"Sure, I'll help you."

.୬ଚ୭.

One day, Anna Joy walked into Harry's office-workroom. He had told her she didn't need to knock anymore, just come in. "Are you ready to look at stereo systems yet?" Harry grinned as he looked up from his plumbing parts catalog.

"I don't know if I have enough money."

He closed the book. "Well, it doesn't hurt to look. I've been doing a little research." He got up and grabbed his keys. "Ready to go?" He led the way out to his plumbing truck.

As they entered the store, Anna Joy's eyes widened. So many incredible stereo systems! How would she ever choose? She gravitated toward the few she thought she could afford, listened to the sound, and checked out the features Harry had told her were important. She sighed. They were okay. She scanned the store. Where did Harry go? He was supposed to help her. Then she heard his voice and walked toward the sound.

"This is a nice system." He handed the headphones back to the salesclerk. "Anna Joy, come check out the sound."

She walked over to Harry and allowed him to place the earphones over her head. She closed her eyes and listened to the clear tones, a clarity she had never heard before. "It's wonderful."

"I'll take it." Harry headed to the register, checkbook in hand.

"The girls will be thrilled. Is this a Christmas present? I promise I won't say a word."

"The girls? No, I picked this one out for you."

"But I haven't given you any money."

"We'll worry about that later." He turned toward the stock person. "You can just load those boxes in my truck." Harry smiled at Anna Joy. "Shall we go and get it all set up?"

She rode home in silence, stunned by Harry's extravagant purchase, so out of character for him.

Harry followed her into the house, hauling the huge boxes into her bedroom. Ruby stared after him while Anna Joy shooed the dogs away from his feet.

"Where do you want me to set it up?"

Anna Joy pointed to a corner in her room, desperately hoping there'd be enough room. She watched Harry gently lift each component from its foam-packed box, set it in place, and attach all their respective cords.

"I think you're all set." Harry grinned, seeming to admire his handiwork.

"Thank you so much, Harry. I'll pay you back, I promise."

"Yeah, yeah. Don't worry about it." He waved at her and walked out to his truck.

Anna Joy stared at her new stereo system components: a dual play/record cassette player, a receiver, a turntable, and two of the largest speakers she had ever seen. She dropped in her favorite music tape, slipped the padded earphones over her ears, and adjusted the volume. She closed her eyes, relishing the rich tones. Thank you, Jesus!

Later she assured Gert she would pay them back.

Gert waved her off. "Don't worry about it. Harry may be a tightwad, but as far as he is concerned, there's nothing too good for his Anna Joy."

23.

Charlie

So if you sinful people know how to give good gifts
to your children, how much more will your heavenly
Father give good gifts to those who ask him.

Matthew 7:11 (NLT)

Anna Joy collapsed onto the faded chair and sighed. She had finished cleaning the kitchen and looked forward to a few moments of rest before she prepared supper. Pepper, Ruby's Pomeranian, jumped onto her lap and plastered her face with doggie kisses. Anna Joy giggled as she swiped Pepper's snout away and wiped the dog slobber off her face with the back of her hand. Pepper circled Anna Joy's lap before settling down, stretching her neck so Anna Joy could scratch her chest.

"I love your dogs, Ruby, but I still miss having a cat," Anna Joy said.

Ruby laughed, shaking her head. "I don't know why you think you need a cat when you're surrounded by all these loving balls of fur. But there's a cat show in town this weekend. Why don't you go check it out? Maybe you'll find one you like."

"Really? You're okay with me getting a cat?"

Ruby shrugged. "What's another animal in the house?"

"Thanks!" Anna Joy slipped Pepper off her lap and onto the chair. Pepper glared. "Sorry, Pepper."

With a bounce in her step, she walked over to the phone and called Gert. Gert had designated herself as Anna Joy's best friend and driver, chauffeuring her to church meetings, the grocery store, and her own home when she determined Anna Joy needed a break from cleaning, cooking, and the multiple malodors.

"Of course, I'll take you! I'm always up for a new adventure."

.·ᴐᵉ᷎ᴐ·.

The next weekend, Anna Joy leaned against the wall by the window. She bit her lower lip as she shifted her weight from one foot to the other, scanning the street for her friend's old Buick. *At last!*

"Gert's here. I'll see you later," she called out.

She walked out to the car as fast as her legs and crutches allowed and slid onto the luxury leather seat. Gert's husband believed in purchasing a good quality car, though never a new one.

"Ready?" Gert smiled and headed for the show. "Let's pray you find the right cat." They pulled into the arena, passing rows and rows of fancy cars. Gert pulled up to the front door to let Anna Joy out. "I'll go park and meet you back here."

Men in suits and ties guided women balancing on their stilettos and wearing fashionable hats through the doorway. Anna Joy tried not to stare. It wasn't polite. She surveyed her plain dress and orthopedic shoes. She had nearly scraped a hole through the toe of one shoe. Despite all of her surgeries, she couldn't help still dragging her foot when she walked. *What was I thinking?*

Gert breezed through the doorway. "Are you ready?" Gert cleared a path for them to the ticket window. They entered the arena and sat down.

While the judges inspected cat after cat, breed after breed, Anna Joy stared, mesmerized by the most beautifully groomed felines she had ever seen. Fluffy, long-haired cats, breeds with perfect markings, and her favorite, Siamese cats. The dark brown markings on their faces, ears, and paws bore a sharp contrast to their cream-colored bodies.

The program stated there were cats available for purchase. After watching the judging for a while, Anna Joy turned to Gert. "Let's go find the area where the cats are for sale."

On arrival, Gert peeked into the room and wrinkled her nose. "I'll wait out here for you." She had an aversion to dirt and odors. Even when she gave Anna Joy rides, she never stepped into Ruby's home.

Cages of cats lined the room. How would Anna Joy ever choose one?

Up ahead, she spied the most beautiful seal point Siamese cat she had ever seen. She leaned against his cage. "Hi, kitty, kitty. You're so beautiful." He stopped licking his cream-colored fur and looked up at her with his blue eyes.

"You could never afford that cat." A woman in a navy suit had stepped up to the cage.

Startled, Anna Joy pivoted and looked up at the woman with perfectly coiffed hair tucked beneath her wide-brimmed hat. A strand of pearls graced her long neck.

The woman looked down her nose at Anna Joy. "Besides, I'm buying this cat. He's exactly what I need for breeding purposes." She turned and strutted away.

Anna Joy's heart sank as she watched the woman's retreating form. The click of her heels echoed in Anna Joy's ears. She glanced at the information sheet documenting the breed and pedigree. Her jaw dropped. She could never afford this price. Tears welled in her eyes. "I wish I could take you home with me, kitty." Her shoulders sagged as she turned away, but not before she noticed the cat's eyes following her.

Anna Joy nearly ran into the woman approaching her. "I'm sorry. I didn't see you."

The woman smiled. "How do you like my cat?"

"He's beautiful." Anna Joy paused, her eyes lingering on the cat. "But I can't afford him. Besides, that other lady said she's buying him."

The woman laughed. "Would you like him?"

"Oh, yes!"

"Then I'll sell him to you."

Anna Joy looked at the floor. "But I don't have that much money."

"How much do you have?"

Anna Joy mumbled a dollar amount.

"I'll sell him to you for that amount. Do we have a deal?"

Anna Joy's eyes widened as she stared into the owner's smiling face. She couldn't believe what she had just heard. Was this lady practically giving her a show-quality Siamese cat? "I'd love to have him! But what about that other woman?"

"She cares nothing for the animals. I don't like her breeding practices. I would never sell her one of my cats. Besides, I rather enjoy selling this cat out from under her." Her tone became more businesslike as she tilted her head and stared into Anna Joy's eyes. "I only have one stipulation." She pointed her finger at Anna Joy. "If you take this cat, you must neuter him. I will not have you competing against me with this cat or his offspring. Is that a deal?"

"Yes! It's a deal!"

"Let's go and take care of the paperwork." She grabbed the carrier and headed into the room designated for sales. They passed by the woman who had laid claim to the cat.

The woman gasped. Then she pursed her lips and glared at Anna Joy.

Anna Joy's hands fumbled as she pulled the money from her wallet and signed the purchase documents. She couldn't believe God had provided her with such a beautiful prize-winning pet.

"Here you are!" Gert appeared at her side, smiling. "I see you found a cat. What's his name?"

"Charlie." Anna Joy beamed and turned to her benefactor. "Thank you so much."

"You're welcome." She bent over and gathered up all her paperwork. "I know you'll take good care of him." She gave them a slight nod and strode into the arena.

Gert grabbed the carrier and led the way toward the car. Before placing the cat in the car, she spread out an old blanket over the back seat.

Anna Joy kept turning around to admire Charlie. "You're such a pretty kitty. I can't believe you're mine."

At Ruby's, Gert carried the cat carrier and set it inside the door for Anna Joy.

"Thank you so much, Gert!"

Gert laughed and waved as she headed back to her car. "My pleasure!"

"Ruby, look! Isn't he the most beautiful cat you've ever seen?" Anna Joy sat down and opened the carrier. Charlie meowed as she picked him up and cuddled him. She scratched behind his ears. He purred and settled onto her lap. "I can't believe God gave you to me."

24.

Spiders and Pests

But in my distress I cried out to the LORD; yes, I
prayed to my God for help. He heard me from his
sanctuary; my cry to him reached his ears.

Psalm 18:6 (NLT)

Anna Joy replaced the phone in its cradle and turned to Ruby. "I got the job!" She rocked back in her chair. After months of seeking employment, she couldn't wait to start her new position.

On her first day of work, Anna Joy awoke early, too excited to eat breakfast. With a lightness in her step, she walked into the pest exterminator's office. She loved phone work—answering calls and scheduling appointments. But she hadn't counted on their prime extermination project—spiders.

She hated spiders, especially the jumping ones. She had nearly leaped out of a moving vehicle when a spider dropped down on the dashboard in front of her. Without her glasses, she couldn't see any object in the distance. But she could spot a speck on the ceiling if it resembled an eight-legged arachnid. As much as she enjoyed living in the Southwest, she wasn't prepared for the multiple species of oversized spiders.

Anna Joy's supervisor oriented her to the new position and led her to a nearby desk.

She slipped into the chair, reached for the phone, and recoiled. A glass-encased tarantula—one leg up and stopped in motion—graced the corner of the desk.

Her supervisor chuckled. "Don't worry. He won't hurt you. We embalmed him with our pesticides. He makes a great paperweight, don't you think?"

Anna Joy gulped. She reconciled the presence of her boss's victory trophy by continually reminding herself that this disgusting creature could never take a step in her direction.

.ᴄᴕᴇᴐ.

Anna Joy enjoyed the company of her office coworkers and the exterminators who popped in on occasion and displayed their pickled pests. One day, her supervisor introduced her to Vanessa, a new employee with long, black-dyed hair. He directed her to the desk next to Anna Joy. "Anna Joy, I'd like you to meet Vanessa, your new coworker."

Anna Joy smiled. "Hi! It's nice to meet you. Let me know if I can help you."

Vanessa glanced toward Anna Joy and smirked. Her short skirt rode up as she leaned in toward the supervisor and gazed into his eyes. "I'll be sure to let you know if I need anything."

Her supervisor thrust his chest out and grinned.

.ᴄᴕᴇᴐ.

"Anna Joy, there seems to be money missing from the cash box. You wouldn't happen to know anything about that, would you?" Vanessa walked past Anna Joy and flashed her a smile.

"I don't understand. I counted the money yesterday, and it was all there." Anna Joy furrowed her brow. As an office worker, she helped oversee the petty cash box. She felt sure she'd calculated the total correctly. After all, she was very good with numbers.

"Well, maybe you just miscounted." Vanessa lifted her arms into the air and shrugged her shoulders. "Or it just disappeared."

Over the course of time, small amounts of money vanished from the cash box. Vanessa continued to accuse Anna Joy of stealing with veiled accusations. "You have so many people to buy groceries for. Did you have enough money this week? I'm sure you can use some extra cash from time to time."

Anna Joy didn't know what to do. How does one respond when not directly accused? She felt responsible for the cash box even though she hadn't stolen the money. Besides, how did Vanessa know she purchased all the groceries with her own money?

Anna Joy prayed and asked God what to do. She sensed the Lord telling her not to defend herself, but to keep silent. She didn't understand why, but she knew the Lord well enough to listen.

One day, when all the other employees were out on calls, Vanessa passed by Anna Joy's desk and opened her hand in front of Anna Joy's face.

Anna Joy jumped back and shrieked.

"You're not afraid of these little ol' spiders, are you?" Vanessa leered. "They won't hurt you."

How did she know spiders terrified Anna Joy? After that incident, living and dead spiders sporadically appeared on her desk.

Day after day, Vanessa harassed Anna Joy, but only when they were alone in the office. Even though Vanessa appeared quite diligent when their boss was around, Anna Joy found herself completing Vanessa's work.

Eventually the day-in-day-out torment siphoned Anna Joy's strength, energy, and joy. The job she once loved knotted her stomach and vexed her spirit. She decided to resign. She left work in tears and headed to the church, hoping for comfort from Sister Gladys.

"What brings you here, Anna Joy? Aren't you supposed to be at work?"

Anna Joy sobbed as she poured out her struggles at work with Vanessa.

Sister Gladys listened as she usually did, one ear tuned to Anna Joy and the other ear tuned to God. "You stop your crying and march right back in there and stand up to this woman. This is the Enemy trying to drive you out. You cannot back down to her. You have authority in Jesus's name. Watch and see what God will do."

Anna Joy sniffled. Where was the motherly comfort she expected? She knew Sister Gladys could be harsh at times, but she hadn't expected such an unsympathetic response. She bit her lower lip, grabbed her crutches, and trudged back into the office.

"Where have you been? A little long for a lunch hour, don't you think?" Vanessa held up her watch and smirked. "Crying to Sister Gladys again? I know you talk to her."

Anna Joy hunched over her desk, avoiding Vanessa's taunting gaze. Her hands shook as she fumbled through the papers in her file. How did Vanessa know she went to see Sister Gladys? Had the Enemy put her in this job just to torment her like Sister Gladys had said? Anna Joy tried to be brave, but she had never encountered this level of opposition before.

.ᴄᴏᴇᴏ.

One morning, Anna Joy steeled her nerves for another day of work with Vanessa. However, when she walked into the office, she noticed Vanessa's desk was cleared and empty.

Confused, she slipped into her chair. She glanced up as her supervisor walked in. "Is Vanessa not coming in today?"

"Nope. I fired her." He crossed his arms, pursed his lips, and stared down his nose at Anna Joy. "I know you didn't steal the money from the cash box. I knew it was her all along. What I don't understand is why you didn't come in and talk to me about what was going on."

Anna Joy licked her lips but remained silent.

He walked toward his office, then turned around. "By the way, you're doing a great job."

Anna Joy smiled. "Thanks!" She sucked in a deep breath. The air had never felt so clean. "Thank you, Jesus." God had taken care of her just like Sister Gladys said he would.

25.

Wrong Way

You see me when I travel and when I rest at home. You know everything I do.

Psalm 139:3 (NLT)

Anna Joy slipped behind the wheel of her mini electric car. She loved the freedom and independence she experienced from being able to drive. Between ice, snow, and cold, she could never drive this battery-operated vehicle up north.

She looked forward to spending an evening at the home of one of her friends. Sometimes they spent evenings in coffee houses featuring various Christian artists. Other times they talked for hours in diners, went to movies, or even visited an occasional theme park. It had been a long time since she had friends her own age to laugh and hang out with. The best part—they loved and accepted her as part of their group.

Since forty-five miles per hour was the vehicle's maximum speed, Anna Joy stayed on the side streets. She felt confident she could find her destination even though she had no sense of direction. After all, this wasn't the first time visiting her friend's home.

She tootled down one side street after another, but before long she realized she was in a part of town she didn't recognize. Rows of paint-chipped houses with crumbling porches lined the narrow roads marked with unfamiliar street signs. Anna Joy bit her lower lip. She was lost. She debated whether she should stop and ask for directions. But her heart raced as she scanned the neighborhood, searching for a friendly face. The only signs of life were a couple of barking dogs zooming across unkempt yards. What should she do now? Even if she could find a pay phone, she couldn't tell anyone where she was.

Up ahead, she spotted several children playing with a ball. She pulled up alongside them and asked if they had heard of the street she was searching for.

The children exchanged glances with one another and shrugged. "Sorry, ma'am. Are you lost?"

She nodded and listed the names of a few main roads, hoping they would recognize one. But they shook their heads.

"Can you tell me how to get to a nearby store or gas station?"

Again, they looked at one another and shook their heads.

Anna Joy scanned the area. Dusk encroached upon them. She didn't relish being alone in a dark place, in a not-so-nice neighborhood. Her chest tightened. "It's getting dark. Don't you need to get home?" Anna Joy remembered her own childhood curfew—be home by the time the streetlights came on or face the wrath of Auntie.

"No." They lightly kicked the ball back and forth.

Even in this unfamiliar place, she felt a strange sense of peace and comfort in the presence of these children. She continued to talk with them, hoping someone would walk by who could help her.

After a while, a car pulled up, and Anna Joy heard a familiar voice. "Hey, Wrong Way, we've been looking all over for you!"

"How did you know I was lost?" Her voice cracked as waves of relief rushed over her. "How did you find me?"

"When you didn't show up at the house, we knew you must've taken a wrong turn, and we set out to search for you. Driving in the opposite direction, of course. We figured we'd eventually find you. Come on, you can follow us."

Anna Joy turned to thank the children who had kept her company when she was so frightened. Where were they? She looked up and down the street. They had disappeared.

Had God sent his angels disguised as children to comfort and protect her? What a kind and loving God to surround her with these youngsters when she felt vulnerable, lost, and alone. He knew she would not feel threatened but safe in the presence of children.

Anna Joy followed her friends and arrived safely at her destination, grateful they knew her so well that her late arrival indicated "Wrong Way" had gotten lost again.

26.

The Toll of Toil

Work willingly at whatever you do, as though you were
working for the Lord rather than for people.

Colossians 3:23 (NLT)

Charlie climbed onto Anna Joy's chest, washed her face with his tongue, and meowed. Anna Joy stirred and slid open her heavy eyelids. "Is it morning already, Charlie?" She stroked her kitty's soft coat. "You won't even let me sleep in on a Saturday, you naughty kitty. Hungry?"

Charlie meowed and leaped to the floor.

Anna Joy slipped over the side of the bed and reached for her crutches. She reflected on her past week: a lengthy Sunday morning church service followed by a short break for lunch before the evening service, her full-time job with the pest control company, Wednesday night church, ministering on the prayer team, and practice with her traveling choir.

As much as she loved to worship, she never imagined the choir director would choose her for the traveling choir. She enjoyed the travel, the camaraderie, and the fancy floor-length dresses. The church promoted modesty in opposition to the miniskirt fad.

Friday evening at the coffee house with friends capped her week. She enjoyed the casualness, conversation, and worship. The banter and laughter with friends relaxed and energized her after a busy week.

Anna Joy dressed and then fed Charlie. She checked the clock. Maybe she could start a load of laundry before Gert arrived to take her grocery shopping. She'd spend the afternoon finishing laundry and cooking for the week. She mentally reviewed her menu: a supper fare of soup, meatloaf, and chicken casserole, and for lunch, tuna salad and cold cuts.

Gert arrived, prompt as usual, and they headed to the grocery store. Anna Joy grabbed a cart and tossed her crutches into the basket. She leaned on the handle for support as she pushed the cart up and down the aisles, talking and laughing with Gert. At least best friends helped make mundane tasks fun.

Gert reached up to the top shelf and snagged Anna Joy's usual cereal purchase. In between helping Anna Joy, Gert filled her own cart.

Anna Joy added several cans of chili beans from the shelf.

"Chili this week? Sounds good." Gert paused mid-aisle. "How long are you going to be able to keep this up? You look exhausted. I wish Sister Gladys could find you some help." Gert shook her head and plunked a few cans of chili beans into her already over-flowing cart.

Anna Joy remained silent as she turned down the next aisle. She did feel tired. How could she answer Gert when she had no answers?

When her mother visited, she had complimented Anna Joy on her trim figure. But between prayer, fasting, work, and managing Ruby's household, she had little time or energy to eat. She wondered how long she could keep up this pace.

She had been under the impression that when she found a job, Sister Gladys would find someone else to help Ruby shop, cook, clean, and do laundry. But between the odors and dogs, the church ladies still refused to even come and visit the shut-ins, let alone offer any assistance.

She knew Sister Gladys had tried to get help. But until someone else took over the household responsibilities, what choice did Anna Joy have? Ruby needed help, and God placed her in Ruby's home. She would do her best to care for Ruby and Frank.

Gert carried Anna Joy's groceries into the house, dodging the dogs. She turned and waved as she walked back to her car. "I'll see you tomorrow!"

Anna Joy unpacked the bags, grabbed a pot for the chili, and started cooking for the week. She glanced at the clock. Once she had the soup started, she could launder the clothes she had pre-treated.

Maybe she would have time to curl up on her bed with headphones, cuddle Charlie, and listen to her favorite Christian music artists. That is, if she didn't fall asleep first. Sunday would be another full day and the start of another busy week.

27.

Tangled Spaghetti

Why, my soul, are you downcast? Why so disturbed within me? Put your hope in God, for I will yet praise him, my Savior and my God.

Psalm 42:11 (NIV)

"You stupid idiot!" Anna Joy berated herself once again. She trudged back to her chair. Her cheeks burned as she sat down and lowered her head onto her desk. She had tried so hard to get to the bathroom on time. Once again, her spastic bladder betrayed her. Hopefully she'd be dry soon. She had almost gotten fired from one job because of too many bathroom breaks. She didn't want to lose her pest control job too.

Her mother kept telling her to go to a doctor. But she had reservations since her multiple childhood surgeries never delivered the promised results. Maybe here she could find a Christian doctor who specialized in kidney and bladder problems, and he could do something to stop the accidents. She would ask Sister Gladys. She must be desperate if she was willing to allow a doctor to probe her insides again.

.༄༅.

"Anna Joy?" A nurse clad in white with a clipboard in her hand stood in the doorway of the doctor's office.

Anna Joy adjusted her crutches and followed the nurse down the hall into an exam room.

"Do you need help changing into a gown?" The nurse pulled a gown out of the drawer and handed it to Anna Joy.

She shook her head.

As the door closed behind the nurse, the small room seemed to close in around her. Memories of previous doctor visits flooded her mind like one continuous motion picture. She didn't like doctors' offices any more now than she did when she was a child. Maybe this time would be different. Hopefully this doctor could help her.

A knock at the door signaled the arrival of the urologist. An older gentleman with a white beard that nearly matched his lab coat walked in. He sat down on a stool next to Anna Joy. "What can I do for you?"

Anna Joy flushed. Even though his eyes seemed warm and welcoming, she avoided his gaze. She told him about the bladder accidents that had plagued her since childhood. After she finished, she looked up at the doctor. "Can you help me?"

"The first thing we need to do is schedule a cystoscopy. We'll slide a scope into your bladder and take a look around. We'll also be able to check your ureters.

"Will it hurt?"

"Since your muscles are spastic and tight from cerebral palsy, we'll give you a general anesthetic. You won't feel a thing." He smiled and patted her hand. "Let's get you scheduled."

.⸱୧ℓ୨⸱.

A woman dressed in hospital scrubs and a bouffant scrub hat approached Anna Joy in the surgical suite. "I'll be the anesthesiologist for your procedure today. Someone told me you hate needles."

Anna Joy studied the woman and instinctively pulled her arm away. "My skin doesn't like needles. They bounce off."

"I promise I will get your IV in with one try. I'm the best there is." The doctor flashed a smile. "Can I take a look at your arm?"

Anna Joy studied the anesthesiologist's face as she slowly extended her arm toward the doctor.

"Make a fist for me."

Anna Joy squeezed her eyes shut as the doctor gently stroked and tapped her arm with her fingers. The tourniquet tightened. She screwed up her face and clutched the bedclothes with her remaining hand. "Did you get it?"

"All done! I promised I would get your IV in on the first try." The doctor placed the last strip of tape over the IV and secured the needle in place.

Anna Joy slid one eye open and then the other and stared at her arm. "No one has been able to start an IV on me in one try." The corners of her mouth slipped into a smile. "Thank you!"

"You're welcome. I'll see you in surgery. We'll take good care of you." The doctor collected her equipment and walked out the door.

.⚬ℓℯ⌐.

Searing pain in her pelvis jarred Anna Joy awake. She groaned. Her eyelids seemed anchored with sleep.

A voice materialized near her. "Anna Joy, are you awake? You're in the recovery room. How are you feeling? The doctor will be in shortly and let you know what he found."

"I hurt really bad. My stomach doesn't feel so good either." She tried to turn her head toward the voice, but her stomach roiled its objection.

"I'll get some medication for you."

Anna Joy wasn't sure how long she slept before the surgeon's voice roused her. She tried to open her eyes and focus, but that proved difficult between the drugs and having no glasses.

The surgeon sat down next to her and reached through the bedrail for her hand. "They'll take you to your room shortly, but I want to talk with you first."

Anna Joy held her breath. Had he been able to help her?

"When I inserted the scope into your bladder, I found multiple areas of scarring, probably from frequent infections. Which we expected. But your bladder is smaller than normal, almost child-sized. It also retains urine, so it doesn't completely empty. That's why you feel like you have to go to the bathroom all the time. Your ureters are also small and scarred. The back pain you've experienced is probably from kidney infections." The doctor paused and pursed his lips.

"I'm sorry, Anna Joy. There was nothing I could do for you."

Anna Joy looked down at her trembling hands. "You weren't able to fix anything?" Her voice barely detectable. "I'll still have the accidents?"

The surgeon squeezed her hand and nodded. "I'm sorry, Anna Joy. You'll probably experience some pain and bleeding for a few days. You can take some over-the-counter pain meds." He paused. "It's important that you drink a lot of fluids to flush out your kidneys and bladder to minimize the recurrence of infections. I am truly sorry."

Just what she needed. More fluids meant more bathroom trips. As she turned away, a tear escaped and dropped on her pillow.

.⟳⟲.

Anna Joy looked forward to the upcoming healing conference. A last hope since the surgery didn't help her. The conference featured world-renowned healing ministries.

Cars with license plates from all over the tri-state area and beyond crammed the parking lot. As the crowd flocked into the building, Anna Joy joined them in search of a seat. She wondered if they, too, were hoping and praying that they would receive a miracle.

As the last chord from the praise and worship faded, a holy hush settled over the auditorium. Testimony after testimony of God's healing power buoyed her faith. She took a deep breath. How much longer? Please God, let today be the day.

The leaders called for those who wanted healing prayer to step forward. Anna Joy slipped out of her seat and joined the throng of people passing her by, pressing their way to the front for prayer. She leaned on her crutches, shifting her weight from one foot to the other, waiting her turn.

Finally, she stood face-to-face with one of the preachers known for a healing anointing. He laid his hands on her head and prayed. Suddenly he withdrew his hands and stepped back. He stroked his chin as if studying Anna Joy. His eyes seemed to bore a hole into her insides.

Anna Joy bit her lower lip. *What does he see?*

He bent his six-foot frame. His eyes brimmed with compassion as he locked eyes with hers and whispered, "Your insides are a mess. They look like a mass of tangled spaghetti. I can't differentiate one organ from another." He paused. "I don't know how you're alive."

Tangled spaghetti? "What do you mean? Can't you pray that God will . . ." She paused. "Untangle me?"

"I'll pray. But I sense that you will need ongoing prayer for healing when you go back home." He laid his hands on her head once again and prayed.

As she stepped out of the arena, the warm air blasted her tear-stained face. The heaviness of another disappointment weighed on her chest. Once again, her hopes and dreams lay at the altar of unanswered prayer.

28.

The Red Dress

"The LORD gave, and the LORD has taken away;
Blessed be the name of the LORD."

Job 1:21 (NKJV)

Anna Joy fingered the red dress she had laid over the chair the night before. Was last night a dream? No. The dress appeared scorched as if a hot iron had seared the fabric.

.∽◦°◦∽.

The previous day, Anna Joy had slipped her red dress off the hanger in anticipation of that evening's church service. The members had fasted and prayed for a fresh move of God, which would culminate in this evening's meeting.

Anna Joy walked up the aisle to a seat near the front. The atmosphere buzzed with electricity. Yes, tonight promised to be special.

The instruments initiated the call to worship. Anna Joy joined the chorus, raising her hands in praise. The voices seemed magnified. Had a heavenly choir joined the congregation?

With each wave of God's presence, she felt strength infuse into her body. Tingles raced up and down her spine and legs. Every cell in her body burned as if on fire.

Anna Joy heard a voice whisper in her ear. "Run!"

She turned to see where the voice was coming from.

The voice whispered again, "Run!"

Obeying the voice, Anna Joy had picked up her crutches and stepped into the aisle. Placing one crutch in front of the other, she scooted forward at a half-run, half-walk pace. She had never moved so fast. The next thing she knew, she dropped her crutches and ran. She wasn't sure her feet even touched the ground as she raced around the room, flinging her arms wide. Unfettered. No crutches. No handicap. Free!

For the next hour as the worship continued, she ran round and round the church without stopping. Then she heard the voice whisper again. "You're tired. Sit down."

Maybe she was a little tired. Her heart pounded as she dropped into her seat, gasping for air. Tears rolled down her flushed cheeks. Heat radiated from her sweat-soaked body. Gratitude and praise poured from her lips. God had healed her!

As the meeting drew to a close, Anna Joy heard a voice whisper, "Pick up the crutches."

No! Surely, she heard wrong.

"Pick up the crutches." The voice whispered, "It's not time yet."

A respected elder approached her, his eyes filled with compassion. His tone was quiet and gentle. "It's not yet time, Anna Joy."

Anna Joy choked back a sob. Her hands trembled as she reached for the crutches. Someone must have laid them on the floor next to her. As she struggled to stand, a heaviness settled over her legs. The healing she desired more than anything else had become tangible. But like a puff of air, her miracle escaped her grasp.

.୧ୋଡ଼ୋ.

Anna Joy slipped the red dress over a hanger and walked to the closet. As she stretched her arm toward the back of the closet, charley horses raced up and down her scarred legs, a screaming reminder that she had overtaxed her muscles. She knew she would never be able to wear that red dress again. But she didn't care. The red dress reminded her of that one hour of freedom from the crippling effects of cerebral palsy. Just as the heat radiating from her body had supernaturally scorched her red dress, so the healing power of God was seared in her memory.

A voice in her spirit interrupted her thoughts. "Do you want to be healed more than you want me?"

"Lord, you know I want you more."

Anna Joy had witnessed countless other people turn away from the Lord after they received the healings they desired. She knew this saddened him. But she also knew if God had healed her, she, too, might have walked away from him. Though crushed by disappointment, she experienced his comforting peace.

Anna Joy echoed Job's prayer. "The LORD gave, and the LORD has taken away; Blessed be the name of the LORD" (Job 1:21 NKJV).

Though she'd experienced only a brief liberation from the restrictions of her handicap, she would forever cherish this gift of freedom—a promise of what was yet to come. Whether in this life or in heaven, she would one day dance and run with joyful abandon.

29.

Southern Goodbyes

*"I will say to the north, 'Give them up!' And to
the south, 'Do not keep them back!'"*

Isaiah 43:6 (NKJV)

Anna Joy opened her Bible and pulled out the bookmark that marked her place in her daily readings—Isaiah 43. She loved how God had made this chapter so personal for her. "Fear not, for I have redeemed you; I have called you by your name; You are Mine" (Isaiah 43:1 NKJV). Yes, she belonged to Jesus.

She read on, "Since you were precious in My sight, You have been honored, And I have loved you" (v. 4). Jesus loved *her*! She was precious to him. Anna Joy had never felt precious to anyone. She continued reading aloud. "I will say to the north, 'Give them up!' And to the south, 'Do not keep them back!'" (v. 6).

As she started to read the next line, she sensed the Lord stop her. She heard a whisper in her spirit, "It's time to go home."

But this was her home. She couldn't have heard correctly. She read again, "And to the south, 'Do not keep them back!'" Surely God was not asking her to leave Sister Gladys, Ruby, Gert, the church, and all her friends. She felt as though her heart would stop beating.

How could the God who loved her so much ask her to leave? She closed her Bible. She needed to talk to Sister Gladys.

.·ево·.

"Oh, Anna Joy! The Enemy is just harassing you. Don't worry. You belong here. This is your home now." Sister Gladys shook her head and laughed.

Anna Joy exhaled the breath she hadn't realized she'd been holding. Her shoulders relaxed. Of course, Sister Gladys was right. God had brought her here, and this was her home.

.·ево·.

But the words "Do not keep them back" wove in and out of her mind like a cobweb she couldn't brush away. She was too busy working at the pest control company, spending time with friends, shopping with Gert, praying with Sister Gladys, and caring for Ruby and Frank to be bothered by these nagging thoughts.

Besides, Sister Gladys had assured her this was her home.

.·ево·.

Anna Joy didn't want to leave. But because the thought of moving niggled in the back of her mind, she sought out Sister Gladys several times for counsel and prayer. Each time, Sister Gladys reminded her that this was her home. Besides, Anna Joy wasn't ready to leave. She still had much to learn and needed continued prayer for healing.

One day after work, the pressure in her chest refused to relent. She had to talk to Sister Gladys. She walked into the church and spotted her at the altar.

"I've been expecting you, Anna Joy." But she wasn't smiling.

"I think God wants me to move back home."

Sister Gladys nodded and prayed with her. "The Lord says it's time for you to go home. We can't hold you back."

"But I don't want to go." Tears streamed down her face. "I don't think I can survive without you. You've helped me so much."

Sister Gladys cradled Anna Joy's hands in her own, a rare gesture of affection. "Honey, when God is telling you to go, you're ready. Even when you don't feel ready. I have taught you everything I know about Jesus and prayer. You have learned by watching me and ministering alongside me. You have the same discernment and giftings I have. I know you've been tired and worn out for a long time. I'm sorry I couldn't find help for you with Ruby and Frank, but I know God honors your faithfulness. You'll be okay." She embraced Anna Joy in a prolonged hug. "I will miss you."

Anna Joy tried to swallow the lump in her throat, but the ache wouldn't allow the grief to pass. Heaviness weighted her legs as she raised herself from the pew and trudged out of the church. She needed to tell Ruby. She knew the news would break her heart. Since Ruby had been unable to bear children, she considered Anna Joy the daughter she'd never had.

.ᴏᴈᴈᴏ.

Anna Joy took a deep breath as she walked through the door of the house she'd considered home for the past eight years. She glanced at the windowsill, wishing Charlie could once again greet her and meow his displeasure at her tardiness.

She smiled as she remembered how Ruby would shake her head in a huff. "That cat has not moved since he got off your bed to wait for you to come home. He won't have anything to do with me while you're gone, but he sure knows when you're supposed to arrive."

But one day, after Charlie had scooted out the door, a neighbor found him lying along the side of the road. As they drove to the veterinary clinic, Anna Joy buried her tear-stained face in Charlie's creamy fur and prayed between sobs. But the doctor had cradled Charlie in his hands and shook his head.

Ruby's greeting pulled her thoughts back to her new sorrow.

"You're late today, Anna Joy." Ruby looked up from the couch.

"I have something I need to tell you, Ruby." Anna Joy sat down, wishing for the comfort of Charlie's cuddles. After a deep breath, she told Ruby about her struggle the past year with the word from the Lord and her times of counsel and prayer with Sister Gladys.

As Ruby listened, tears glistened in her eyes. "I knew we couldn't keep you here forever. I'll miss you."

Anna Joy nodded. "I'll miss you too. I'm so grateful you gave me a home when I had nowhere else to go."

.⸴ঙ৶৹.

Anna Joy knew her leaving would also create a void in Gert's life, especially since her girls were growing up and leaving for college. A few sniffles escaped as Gert helped Anna Joy pack her bags. She carefully folded each garment and laid them in the suitcases so they wouldn't wrinkle.

Anna Joy reminisced about how her kitty used to jump in and out of her bags when she packed for a trip, determined to go with her.

Harry packed her stereo system in the original boxes he had saved in case she ever needed them. He would take care of shipping the items she couldn't take on the plane. She knew how much he would miss the one person who listened to him, even when she didn't understand the technical aspects of his work. His silence spoke volumes.

Anna Joy picked up the paperweight gifted to her as a going-away present from her pest control friends. She grimaced as she examined the encased critter and set it back down. Maybe she would leave this gift behind. She had enjoyed the camaraderie of her coworkers, even the exterminators, who occasionally shared with her their latest conquest.

She blinked back tears. Would she be able to find another job?

30.

A New Beginning

In their hearts humans plan their course, but
the LORD establishes their steps.

Proverbs 16:9 (NIV)

Anna Joy locked the door of the flat she shared with her mother, walked to the stairs, and tossed a crutch down the steps. She grasped the rail with one hand, and, with the other, placed her remaining crutch on the next stair and stepped down. At the bottom of the steps, though hindered by the bulkiness of her coat, she picked up her crutch. The porch light cast shadows across the snow-packed ground. She stepped off the porch, steeling herself against a blast of arctic air. Since moving back north, she hadn't yet adjusted to the dark mornings and bitter cold winters.

She walked around to the front of the building and waited for the paratransit bus that would transport her to her job at the downtown bank. Anna Joy scheduled an early bus time so she wouldn't be late for work. The wind whipped around her legs and tugged at her hood. Hopefully, the bus would arrive soon. Before long, the faint glow of headlights shone through her fogged glasses.

The bus picked up a few more passengers before dropping her off in front of the bank. She balanced herself against the marble wall of the building, grasped her mitten between her teeth, and pulled it off. Her mitten dangled from her mouth as she fumbled with the key to unlock the door. Thankfully, one of the vice presidents had ordered a key for her after he noticed Anna Joy waiting each morning by the door when he arrived early to open.

She locked the door behind her, walked behind the reception desk, and draped her coat over the special office chair they had provided. After stowing her purse beneath the desk, she reached for the watering can she kept in the corner. She crooned over the violets gracing the ledge of her desk, adding water to their saucers. The clock indicated she would have time to head to the employee breakroom. There'd be plenty of time for Bible reading and prayer before her workday began.

⋅⌒⊙⌒⋅

Months earlier, Anna Joy had answered a job posting from the bank seeking a receptionist and scheduled an interview.

At the designated time, she walked into the bank and followed an employee into the office of one of the vice presidents. "I'm here to apply for the receptionist job."

He looked up from his work and motioned for her to take a seat. "The job entails sitting at the front desk, managing the switchboard, and directing customers to the appropriate department. Is this something you think you can do?"

Anna Joy nodded. "I worked for almost eight years as a receptionist for a pest control office. Before that, I was a switchboard operator for the telephone company." She tried to sound self-assured, but she knew the odds of a company hiring an employee with a disability were slim.

After discussing the position in more detail, the manager cocked his head to one side and paused. "All right, we'll give you the job. There's a three-month probationary period. I'll have someone take you to Human Resources. We can complete the paperwork there and order you some uniforms. You can start next week."

.ৡৡৣ.

Between phone calls, Anna Joy greeted the bank customers. Many regulars stopped by her desk to chat, welcomed by her friendly smile. As part of her job, she managed a petty cash box and sold stamps. After she balanced the account at the end of the day, the head teller collected the box, locked it in the safe, and then returned it to her desk the next morning. Anna Joy had always been good with numbers. Before long she had memorized every extension on the switchboard.

She didn't find out until later how God intervened on her behalf. The vice president in charge of hiring had been unavailable on the day of her interview. When he discovered his associate had hired Anna Joy, he expressed his displeasure. He said a "crippled woman" did not meet his criteria for the first person a customer encountered when they arrived at his institution. Maybe he could replace her before she completed her probation. But the other vice president, who hired her, was pleased with her work and her melodic voice when she paged the employees over the intercom system.

.ৡৡৣ.

In the evenings, while her mother watched television programs, Anna Joy often retired to her space in a corner of the living room that contained her desk stacked with her stereo components. She sat down in her office chair, placed the headphones over her ears, and lost herself in praise and worship. Her one semblance of privacy. She was grateful her mother had adjusted her living space in the one-bedroom apartment. At Anna Joy's request, she replaced her double bed with twin beds. Anna Joy did not wish to repeat her childhood sleeping in the same bed with her mother.

31.

An Unforeseen Twist

Trust in the LORD with all your heart; do not depend
on your own understanding. Seek his will in all you
do, and he will show you which path to take.

Proverbs 3:5-6 (NLT)

"I'm praying that the Lord will lead you to a Christian community, Anna Joy." Sister Gladys's words echoed in Anna Joy's ears after she hugged her goodbye. But she shrugged off the concern she heard in Sister Gladys's voice. She already knew which fellowship she would attend.

Before moving eight years ago, she had attended a home Bible study group. She looked forward to reconnecting with the leaders who faithfully drove across town to pick her up each week. Since she'd left, the group had outgrown its home, and her leader had become the senior pastor of the larger fellowship group.

.⊶⊷.

Anna Joy walked through the door of the now-established church and scanned the room, searching for a familiar face.

"Anna Joy! It's so good to see you! Back for a visit?" The greetings poured forth from those who remembered her and warmed her heart.

"I'm not visiting this time. I've moved back."

As she worshipped, she felt at home, almost as if she'd never left. Sister Gladys didn't need to worry. She had found her new church family.

.୨ٯٯ.

In order to participate in the community social activities and small groups, one needed to become a member of the fellowship. As a prospective member, Anna Joy was required to meet with the elders. She wasn't concerned about this meeting. After all, she was a founding member of the fellowship group.

She sat down with the pastor and his wife. "I'm so happy to be here, to see everyone. I'm looking forward to being a part of this community again."

The pastor exchanged glances with his wife before clearing his throat. "You know we are thrilled to see you, Anna Joy, and we're so glad you're doing well. It's obvious the Lord has worked much healing in your life."

Anna Joy stiffened. Something was wrong.

"I know this may be difficult for you to understand, but we do not sense that the Lord is calling you to be part of our fellowship."

A chill swept through the room. Anna Joy shivered. *What are they saying? I don't belong here? I was a founding member.*

"You're more than welcome to worship with us on Sunday mornings and participate in all of our public events. But we are not able to offer you any small group fellowship or participation in our closed community activities."

Besides banning her from all social activities, she knew their strict fellowship policies would forbid her from spending time with her best friend, her only friend, outside of Sunday services. If they violated the rules, they would both be ostracized. How could they apply these policies to her?

"We believe God is calling you to another place, and we do not wish to hinder his plans for you or the community he is calling you to. I'm sorry, Anna Joy."

Another church? But this was her home.

Anna Joy stumbled out the door, tears clouding her vision. How could God be calling her to another place? What place? She'd already lost one church family, and now he was asking her to give up another church family. Her mother would never understand, let alone forgive, the Christians who rejected her daughter. Even if she didn't tell her, her mother would know something was wrong when Anna Joy no longer spent time with her best friend or attended the fellowship.

.⊶⊷.

One day, Anna Joy sensed the Lord leading her to go to a Catholic prayer group meeting. Though raised Catholic, she no longer attended a Catholic Church. Why would God want her to visit a Catholic prayer group?

She walked down the stairs of the Catholic Center and entered a large room with folding chairs arranged in a circle. She sat down in a chair near the door, close enough for a quick getaway. Dissonant notes drifted toward her as the musicians tuned their guitars in a corner.

While she watched the members of the prayer group trickle in, Anna Joy's eyes widened. Men in muscle shirts and women with halter tops wrapped their arms around each other in warm embraces. Their cutoffs barely covered their behinds. This lack of clothing and freedom of affection between the sexes would never have been tolerated in her previous fellowship.

She reached for her crutches. Maybe she could scoot out the door before anyone noticed her. She didn't belong here. One of the men in cutoffs sat down next to her. His long hair, though thinning on top, extended the length of his scraggly beard. As he introduced himself, he offered her a folder that fell open to a page of typewritten lyrics. *Jesus, help me!*

The strum of guitars opened the meeting with praise and worship. Strains of unfamiliar melodies filled the room. Between songs, someone read a Scripture, another shared a word from the Lord, and another a testimony. After prayer requests and a closing song, the meeting ended.

As conversation buzzed around her, Anna Joy reached for her crutches. Her hands trembled. She focused her gaze on the quickest escape route. Tears streamed down her cheeks as she hurried toward the door.

A man wearing jeans and a T-shirt slipped in front of her, blocking her exit. She looked up into the face of one of the prayer meeting leaders.

"Hi there. What's your name?" The tall thin man stroked his chin.

"Anna Joy." She swiped her tears with the back of her hand and tried to maneuver around him. "Excuse me. I'm leaving."

"I think we have a small group that would be a good fit for you. Would you be interested?"

Whether from embarrassment or anger, Anna Joy felt her cheeks flush. Even though his voice seemed gentle and kind, how dare he assume she needed a group, especially one he provided. "No. I'm not coming back."

"Let me give you my number. Call if you change your mind." He fished through his pockets, pulled out a scrap of paper and a pen, and wrote his name and number. "I hope you'll reconsider." He handed her the paper and stepped aside.

Anna Joy crumbled the paper in her hand and looked around for a trash can. Finding none, she shoved the scrap in her purse.

.⊙⊰⊱.

"Lord, why do you keep nagging me about this prayer group? How can you ask me to be a part of a group of people who lack any propriety regarding their conduct and their dress?"

"They need you." The voice in her spirit paused. "And you need them."

Anna Joy snorted. "I don't think so! I'm not going back."

She wrestled with God over the course of several months regarding the prayer group. At last, she relented.

"All right! I'll attend the small group. One time. But I'm not going to the larger meetings."

.ᴼᴸᵉ.

Anna Joy fidgeted in the kitchen chair, waiting for her ride to the small group meeting. She had not met the woman who would drive her, but she sounded nice enough on the phone. Besides, she worked for the sheriff's department. How bad could she be?

The woman arrived professionally dressed and wearing a friendly smile. Though not particularly chatty, she allowed Anna Joy to glean a few tidbits about her and the group she hosted. The woman shared her home with a part wolf, part German Shepherd guard dog. Anna Joy surmised that maybe the group was okay since the attendees included an employee of the sheriff's department, a couple of medical students, and a nun.

Across the room sat a university PhD student, Allen, who she recognized as the bearded man who sat next to her at the prayer meeting. She later learned he was the only one who attended the large group meeting on a regular basis.

The members welcomed her, but thankfully, they didn't pepper her with lots of questions. The wounds inflicted by her old fellowship still oozed with the pain of rejection and betrayal.

The evening passed quickly, almost too quickly, and proved enjoyable—to Anna Joy's surprise. She agreed to meet with the small group weekly, as long as she didn't have to attend the larger prayer meetings.

32.

The Retreat

And yet, O LORD, you are our Father, We are the clay, and
you are the potter. We all are formed by your hand.

Isaiah 64:8 (NLT)

"I don't want to go to this prayer group retreat, Lord. I thought we had agreed I'd only have to go to the small group. I don't want to go out of town with a bunch of people I don't know."

The week before, Allen sat down next to Anna Joy. "I know you've been praying for me and for the others on the retreat planning team. But I'd like for you to come with us on the retreat."

How dare he ask me to go? He knows how I feel about going to the large group prayer meetings.

Over the many months of meeting with the small group, Allen had not only shaved his beard and cut his hair but also became a trusted friend. He provided her with transportation to their small group, invited her to dinner and worship at the Christian co-op where he lived, and occasionally visited her during her work hours at the bank. His kindness and gentleness had won her over despite his unconventional appearance.

Anna Joy curled her lips. "I can't share a room with people I don't know."

"The retreat will be at a convent, so all the rooms are private. You can ride with me. When we break into small groups, I'll make sure you're in a group with people you know."

The inside of her mouth suddenly dried as she mumbled, "I'll think about it." She wasn't going.

.ༀ.

Anna Joy's stomach lurched as she waited for Allen. She stared at her bag, packed for the weekend retreat. *What was I thinking? I could still back out* . . . the doorbell jarred her thoughts. Allen didn't ask if she was ready. He picked up her bags and carried them to the car while she trailed behind.

For nearly two hours, they drove in silence, her stomach churning with every passing mile. At last they arrived at the sprawling brick complex—her home for the weekend—which overshadowed a manicured lawn bordered by a lake. After she registered and received her room assignment and weekend schedule, Allen escorted her to her room. She tried to pay attention as he consulted the map and gave her directions to all the rooms they would be using over the course of the next few days, but she had no sense of direction. It really didn't matter. She planned to lock herself in the room all weekend.

Allen helped her settle into the room and laid the information packet on her bed. "I'll come back and get you for this evening's session, so you'll know where to go."

She sat down on the only chair in the sparsely furnished room. Her weekend cell included a twin-sized bed, a dresser, a sink, and a bedside table with a nondescript lamp. A crucifix hung on the wall. Definitely a nun's quarters. She pulled out the welcome packet and riffled through the papers: a schedule, name tag, and meeting room for her small group assignment. Allen wouldn't be a part of her group, but at least she knew a couple of the people assigned to it.

The next morning, Anna Joy stood in a puddle of water as she leaned against the sink in the communal bathroom, rinsing her clothes.

A woman from the retreat team, whom she only knew by name, approached her. "Do you need help?"

"No!" Her cheeks burned with embarrassment. "I'm fine." She hadn't meant to sound so harsh, but her bladder had betrayed her once again—in front of everyone.

She skipped breakfast and had just finished dressing when Allen knocked on her door. She allowed him to hand her the crutches. Too bad her arsenal of stalling techniques was limited to generalized slowness. As the door shut behind her, the tapping of her crutches echoed down the corridor. Chatter and laughter drifted into the hallway from the large gathering room. Maybe she could sneak in and hide in a corner.

After worship and a short talk, one of the retreat leaders rose and addressed the group. "This weekend, we've talked about God being the potter and we, the clay. So, on the table, we have paper plates with lumps of clay for each one of you. Form the clay into something that represents you. This evening, we'll offer our creations to God as a symbol of offering ourselves to him."

As if this retreat couldn't get any worse, they were now asking her to sculpt something with spastic cerebral palsy hands. Before she could manage a strategic exit, Allen appeared in front of her with the clay and a bowl of water.

"Would you like to work on this project at a table?" He didn't wait for a response. He sidled up to a table and set down the rudimentary materials.

The gray lump of clay seemed to mock her ability to create a masterpiece. She dipped her hand into the bowl and spread the water over the formless slab. Squishing the cold, wet lump between her fingers reminded her of the many frustrating occupational therapy sessions she had endured. As she rolled and patted the damp slab into a ball, the clay dried like glue on her hands.

That afternoon, Anna Joy watched the other attendees as they admired one another's clay masterpieces. She gazed at the transformed lumps of clay: an angel, a snail, a porcupine, a bird, a tree . . . She turned away, her face flushed with shame. Tomorrow she could go home and forget this humiliating weekend.

During the last evening session, one of the leaders stepped up. "We would like to take some time this evening for each one of us to share how the masterpieces we created with lumps of clay represent us and then offer a prayer dedicating ourselves to God."

One by one, the participants collected their sculptures, shared the significance, and prayed.

When Anna Joy's turn came, she grasped the plate with both hands, afraid she'd drop it and add to her weekend mortification. "I rolled mine into a ball." Her voice quavered. "Lord, I am your plaything, and you can do with me whatever you wish."

The next morning, Anna Joy sat on the couch laughing and chatting with a young man and woman she had met at the retreat. The night before, they had prayed with her for healing from the bladder accidents.

Her bladder had not betrayed her since they'd prayed.

33.

The Amusement Park

He will once again fill your mouth with laughter
and your lips with shouts of joy.

Job 8:21 (NLT)

"Some of us from the prayer group are planning to go to Great America on Saturday. Would you like to go?" Allen walked Anna Joy to the door after their small group meeting.

"Great America? I'd love to go! I want to ride the biggest roller coaster they have." Anna Joy loved amusement parks. It had been a long time since she'd been on an outing with a group of friends, let alone gone to an amusement park. She was going to Great America!

Allen had mentioned a few names, including Debra and the two people who prayed with her on the retreat. She couldn't believe her new prayer group friends were willing to take her to an amusement park, knowing they would have to lift her up onto the rides. She'd have to ask someone if she could borrow a wheelchair.

On Saturday morning, Allen laid the wheelchair in the trunk while she joined the others, piling into his vehicle, laughing and chatting. She'd hardly slept that night, anticipating all the wild rides at Great America. But her new friends made the two-and-a-half-hour drive pass by quickly.

At the amusement park, Anna Joy slipped into the wheelchair. "Let's go find the roller coasters!"

Allen pushed the wheelchair toward the nearest roller coaster, followed by their friends. He lifted her onto a first-row seat and sat next to her while the others climbed in behind them. According to Anna Joy, the front car offered the biggest thrill. She grasped the restraining bar, barely able to tamp down her excitement. The roller coaster lurched forward as it clacked along the track, rapidly picking up speed. The cars raced around a corner, climbed to new heights, plunged, and flipped them upside down, not once but twice. Anna Joy screamed in delight just like her brother taught her years ago after she threw up on her first roller coaster ride. *If you scream, you won't get sick,* she remembered again.

The roller coaster roared into the station and stopped. The attendant walked along the track's edge, lifted the safety bars, and directed passengers to the exit. He stopped by Anna Joy as Allen began to help her out. "Would you like to ride again? We know it's hard for you to get on and off the rides."

"Yes, thanks!" Anna Joy clapped her hands together and plopped back in the seat. Her disability gained her and her friends an extra ride.

After the second go around, Allen lifted her out of the car. "Where to now?"

"How about that roller coaster?" Anna Joy's eyes sparkled as she pointed to a larger and more imposing structure filled with twists and turns. Off she rode in pursuit of new heights and more thrills.

They spun around in the Scrambler, the Tilt-A-Whirl, and all the spinning rides before breaking for lunch. She spied the group crowded on the brick bench encircling one of the few trees in the park. A little shade, a slice of pizza, and a bit of catching up. One woman clutched a stuffed animal she'd won on the midway. But Anna Joy had no use for the midway games when the park offered so many rides.

After lunch, Anna Joy and Allen headed to the cable cars. An aerial ride over the park seemed tame enough post-lunch. Allen lifted her foot into the cabin just as the car pitched, causing her to tumble into the seat. She grabbed the window ledge and pulled herself over, making room for him. As the car swayed along its cable, she hung her head out the window and scanned the grounds. She reveled in the view from above as well as the breeze cooling her warm cheeks.

By afternoon, sweat poured off their brows. When the shade had all but disappeared, Anna Joy suggested they head for the water rides.

Allen wheeled her to the Yankee Clipper, with her new friends in tow. The little boat rocked in the water as Allen lifted her into the first seat of the vessel and then crawled in behind her. The boat started its climb to the highest peak, plummeted, and picked up speed as it wound around the twists and turns. Anna Joy shrieked as the waves washed over the sides of the boat, splashed her in the face, and soaked her clothes. Her clothes would dry soon enough in the August heat. At least she'd cooled down.

Later, even though darkness had descended on the park, Anna Joy wasn't ready to leave yet. She scanned the entertainment complex, its bright lights glowing against the night sky. "I want to ride Logger's Run one more time!"

"But you won't have time to dry off before you go home. You'll be cold." One of her friends piped up.

"I don't care! Let's go!"

Allen pushed her wheelchair to the log ride for one last adventure. The Logger's Run platform turned like a carousel while the riders boarded and disembarked. Allen lifted her into the front seat of the carved-out log and then crawled in behind her. The tracks propelled the log to the top of the structure. Anna Joy clung to the handle and screamed as the log plummeted down its makeshift flume, wound around the sharp turns, and showered her once again with the crashing waves.

After Allen helped her out of the low-riding log, she struggled to maintain her footing on the water-soaked planks of the rotating platform. While he ran for the wheelchair, one friend positioned himself in front of her, holding her outstretched arms, and another stood behind her to prevent her from falling.

Despite being soaked from head to toe and shivering, she grinned as Allen pushed her to the car, followed by the rest of their party. He flipped the car heater on for the drive home. The return trip was much more subdued as the exhausted party settled back in their seats and closed their eyes.

It had been a long time since Anna Joy enjoyed a day with friends. Maybe God had directed her to the right place after all.

34.

Winter Fun

*So I recommend having fun, because there is nothing better
for people in this world than to eat, drink, and enjoy life.*

Ecclesiastes 8:15 (NLT)

"How would you like to come and play broomball with us?" Scott ambled into Anna Joy's apartment, unzipped his heavy winter coat, and sat down next to her.

"Broomball. What's that?"

"We basically play hockey on ice using a broom and a ball. A group of us are playing this afternoon."

"So, I'll be watching?"

Scott laughed. "Oh no. I'm going to pull you behind me on a sled."

Anna Joy shook her head. "You're crazy."

"Maybe. But do you want to come?"

Anna Joy paused. "Okay. I'll have to change clothes."

"I'll wait. Dress warm!"

.ᴐᴏℓᴇᴏ.

As she stepped out of the car, the wind whipped around her face. Anna Joy hoped she would be warm enough. Now bundled in her thick down coat, mittens, and boots, she could barely move. She reached for her crutches.

"You won't need those." Scott pulled a sled out of the car. "Here, let me help you. Just lie down on your stomach. I got you." He adjusted Anna Joy on the sled so no part of her body would drag in the ice and snow. He grabbed the cord, looked back at Anna Joy, and offered her a mischievous grin. "Are you ready?" Before she could answer, he pulled her out onto the ice and joined his friends.

Anna Joy gripped the edge of the sled as best as she could with her down gloves. "Let's go!" She cried out as the blades slid over the ice behind Scott. "Mush!"

A broom whacked the ball. Feet slid and slipped over the icy surface. Brooms brushed over the ice, sweeping the ball to the nearest team member who would then race toward the goal before an opponent could brush the ball away. Rear ends bounced on the ice as the players attempted to keep up the pace or strategically trip their opponents.

Scott somehow managed the broom and stayed on his feet. He flew from one end of the frozen pond to the other with Anna Joy in tow, cheering their team to victory.

"We won!" Anna Joy shrieked.

"How about a game of crack the whip," someone shouted.

A chorus of "Yeahs!" rose. Hand-in-hand, the group formed a whip. Scott and Anna Joy took up the rear.

Between chattering teeth, she whooped as she bounced on the wooden slats of the sled. It felt like her head was spinning as they whipped her around the ice faster and faster. Sometimes she wasn't sure if her sled remained on the ice or flew in the air.

After the game, she waddled through the door of her home, chilled to the bone. Her cheeks cold, reddened, and chafed. Time for a hot bath, warm clothes, and hot chocolate.

The next morning, her bones and muscles ached, as well as muscles she never knew existed. Anna Joy surveyed her body parts that she could see. Splotches of various shades of black and blue overshadowed her pale white skin.

She laughed. She couldn't recall the last time she had so much fun.

.⟶ɷɛ⟵.

More adventures awaited her when one of the prayer group leaders had moved to a house in the country and invited the members to a winter open house. When Allen asked her to go, she reluctantly agreed since she was still getting to know people in the group. But she didn't enjoy big parties.

When they arrived, a group had gathered at the top of a hill. Sleds, saucers, and commandeered cafeteria trays bounced over the snow-packed ridges as they propelled their occupants faster and faster down the hill.

"Watch out for the trees!" Someone at the top of the hill yelled.

Allen turned to Anna Joy. "Would you like to go sledding?"

"I'm not dressed for this." Bundled in her down coat and gloves, she watched the others from the top of the hill. The snow would quickly soak through her pants.

"I brought some snow pants you can wear." Debra approached them from behind. "Let's go back to the house, and I'll help you put them on."

Anna Joy and Debra laughed as they stuffed Anna Joy and her clothes into the snow pants. As Anna Joy waddled outside, the nylon pant legs scraped together with each step. *Schwip. Schwop. Schwip. Schwop.*

Allen positioned her on the sled and then slid behind her. One of their friends shoved the sled, and down the hill they sailed.

Anna Joy screamed with delight. When they reached the bottom of the hill, she turned to Allen. "Can we do it again?"

Allen nodded, grabbed the rope, and pulled her up the hill. They had sledded down the hill several times with Allen pulling her back up to the top.

"Can I go down by myself?"

Allen hesitated, pursing his lips. "Well, you'll probably go a lot faster."

"Oh, good!" With Allen's help, she lay prone on the sled.

"Be careful not to run into the trees. If you start heading toward the trees, you pull this rope in the direction you want the sled to go." He placed the rope in her hands.

"I'm ready. Let's go!"

Allen gave her a push.

Anna Joy slid and bounced over the snow drifts faster and faster. "Whee!"

"Turn the sled! You're heading toward the trees!" Allen ran down the hill, slipping and sliding.

Anna Joy beat him down the hill, unaware she had barely missed a tree. When Allen arrived, she turned her reddened face toward him, oblivious to the cold. "That was a blast!"

The blustery wind and cold finally drove the party indoors. Their sledding adventure ended for the day.

35.

A Little Boy Promise

The LORD always keeps his promises; he is gracious in all he does.

Psalm 145:13 (NLT)

The toddler wandered around the room. He wove around the chairs set up for the prayer meeting, seemingly oblivious to the worship team tuning their instruments or the people mingling about the room, chattering.

As Anna Joy entered the room, the Lord drew her attention to the two-year-old boy. She watched him look up, almost hopeful. But he quickly turned away, face crestfallen. Each time someone entered the room, his eyes darted toward the door. Was he looking for his mother?

Anna Joy's heart broke for him. She knew he had never been separated from his mother for any length of time. But his mother needed to remain in the hospital after delivering a premature baby boy.

Anna Joy sensed the Lord nudge her. *I want you to buy him a present.* She knew new babies often receive lots of gifts, and sometimes the older child feels left out.

The next week, Anna Joy walked over to the little boy. "Hi Joshua, I have a present for you."

His eyes toggled between Anna Joy and the large, wrapped box she held out to him. He didn't seem to know what to do with the gift.

"Open it." She lowered herself onto the floor next to him. She pulled a corner of the paper away from the package. "Like this."

Joshua pulled the paper away, gingerly at first and then ripped the wrapping off the package. His eyes widened as he pulled a wooden train set out of the box. He looked up at Anna Joy. His face beamed.

She had given the little boy a train. But God gave Anna Joy a godson.

.ᴏᴈℓᴇᴐ.

The next year, Anna Joy invited Joshua and his family to her birthday party.

She sat on the floor next to Joshua's mother while opening one of her birthday presents—a bag of Hershey's kisses. "Joshua, come here." She held out a piece of candy for him.

He dropped his toy and walked over to Anna Joy and his mother. He stared at the Hershey's kiss.

"You eat it." She unwrapped a piece and put it in her mouth. "Hm. Good."

He took the piece of candy from her hand and started to put it in his mouth, foil and all.

"We have to take the paper off first." Anna Joy unwrapped the chocolate and put it in his mouth.

He swished it around, scrunched his face, and walked away. A few minutes later he returned and held out his hand. "More."

Anna Joy grinned as she gave him another piece of chocolate.

A short while later, he stood in front of Anna Joy and pointed to the bag. "Can I have it?"

Anna Joy chuckled. "I'll give you one more piece." She handed him another piece of candy. After he left, she hid the bag behind her back, turned to his mother, and chuckled. "I think I created a chocolate monster."

.ново.

While visiting Joshua's mother one day, Anna Joy watched him grasp a wooden hammer and pound another peg into the block. When he finished, he plucked a plastic screwdriver from his toy tool belt. He walked through the living room pressing the screwdriver into various items, pretending to fix things just like his dad.

Joshua walked over and stood in front of Anna Joy. "I want real tools."

Anna Joy furrowed her brow and then glanced at his mom. "Maybe when you're older, we can get you some real tools." What three-year-old asks for real tools?

"No, I want real tools."

Anna Joy prayed about Joshua's request.

She sensed the Lord say, *I want you to give him a tool for every birthday and Christmas until he's twenty-one.*

"Lord, I don't know if I'll still be around until he's twenty-one. How can I make such a promise to a three-year-old?"

The Lord repeated, *I want you to give him a real tool for every birthday and Christmas until he's twenty-one.*

That Christmas, Anna Joy presented Joshua with a large metal toolbox and small hammer. "The Lord told me to give you a real tool for every birthday and Christmas until you're twenty-one. Here's a real toolbox to put all your tools in."

Joshua's eyes widened as he stared at his new toolbox and hammer.

.ново.

Each Christmas and birthday, she added to his toolbox, tools that exceeded even the quality of those owned by his dad.

Anna Joy kept her promise. The Lord's promise to a little boy.

36.

Next Stop, Israel

And God will generously provide all you need.

2 Corinthians 9:8 (NLT)

"Israel?" Anna Joy stared at the couple she barely knew from church. "You want me to go to Israel with you?"

"We've talked about it, and we want you to join our tour."

"You don't even know me." The tour group included middle-aged and older people, most of whom she'd never met. They weren't her prayer group friends who had wheeled her around Great America. "That's a lot of extra work for you. Someone would have to lift me on and off the bus, push me in the wheelchair up the hills and over rocky paths."

"We've talked about it, and we feel the Lord wants you to come with us. The trip just wouldn't be the same without you."

Anna Joy shook her head, stunned that they would want to bother with her. "How much does it cost?" Her mind scanned the possibility. But her salary at the bank barely covered her living expenses. How could she afford such a trip? But *Israel*. She'd always wanted to go to Israel. Maybe if she had lots of time, she could squirrel away a few dollars here and there. "When are you planning to go?"

"Next year. It'll be for three weeks at the end of February. We're also going to Egypt and Jordan. It'll cost about three thousand dollars."

Anna Joy counted the months until their departure—six. "I'll pray about it," she mumbled. Six months to raise the money. Impossible. Plus, there was no way her supervisor would give her that much time off work. It was their busy season, and she only qualified for two weeks of vacation per year.

Anna Joy prayed about the trip, just as she promised the couple. But she found it difficult to pray with any faith. However, the more she prayed, the more she sensed the Lord wanted her to go. How could this be? There's no way she could save $3000 for the trip.

How much money do you have in your savings account?

"Lord, you know I only have three hundred dollars."

What is the tithe on three thousand dollars?

Anna Joy swallowed hard and whispered, "Three hundred dollars."

I want you to give one hundred dollars to three different people. He impressed three names on her heart.

"But Lord, I'm saving this three hundred dollars for the trip."

Do you trust me to provide the money?

"Yes, Lord, I trust you." Anna Joy recalled the times the Lord had faithfully provided for her.

.ᴄ໑໐ᴄ.

One time—before the days of TSA and modern boarding passes—the Lord had told her to get on a plane, even though she had no money. With trepidation, she obeyed, more afraid of disobeying the Lord than being kicked off a plane for lack of fare.

She boarded the bus that would transport the passengers to the prop plane parked on the tarmac. *Lord, I still don't have the money for a ticket.*

She waited until all the passengers got off before grabbing her crutches and stepping down onto the tarmac. The heat radiated off the surface, contributing to the heat rising in her cheeks. She bit her lower lip as she glanced at the plane and hauled herself up the metal steps, trying not to grasp the scorching rail too tightly. She scanned the cabin, searching for a vacant seat, and spotted one in the back. Of course, the only vacant seat would be in the back. She would have to walk all the way down the narrow aisle to the back of the plane. When they found out she couldn't pay, she'd have to walk back down the aisle in front of everyone, humiliated. Sweat poured off her brow as she shuffled to her seat.

The flight attendant started at the front of the plane and collected the tickets from each passenger.

Anna Joy stared at her trembling hands while she waited.

When the attendant arrived at Anna Joy's seat, she studied the passenger list in her hand, looked up, and smiled. "Your fare's been paid. Have a good flight."

Anna Joy blew out the deep breath she hadn't realized she'd been holding. She glanced around, wondering who had paid for her ticket, but she never found out. *Thank you, Lord! I can't believe you did it!*

.ஒஒ.

Memories of God's faithfulness pinged through her mind. Anna Joy withdrew three $100 bills from the bank and gave one to each of the individuals the Lord had named.

She prayed before approaching her supervisor. If the bank wouldn't give her the time off, the trip would end in her supervisor's office.

She drew in a deep breath and knocked on the door. "I was wondering if I could speak with you about my vacation for next year."

Her supervisor motioned for her to have a seat.

Anna Joy explained her vacation request. "I know I only have two weeks of vacation, but I could take a week without pay. I would really love to go to Israel if at all possible."

Her supervisor drummed her fingers on her desk. She tilted her head, seeming to study Anna Joy. "I'll approve your request, on the condition you tell no one about this." She smiled—a rare smile.

"Thank you. I won't say a word. And I'll make sure everything at the switchboard is all set for a sub." Anna Joy turned and walked back to the switchboard. "Thank you, Jesus!"

Little by little, the funds trickled in. Sometimes friends thrust money or checks into her hand or her purse. Other times she came home from work and found twenty-dollar bills stuffed in envelopes with no return address and marked with the Star of David.

When the down payment for her trip was due, Anna Joy rejoiced that she, too, could finalize her reservation. "You did it, Lord! You did it!" God had provided so far. Surely, he would provide the rest of the money. She was going to Israel.

After Christmas, Anna Joy pored over the suggested packing list and itinerary for the trip. She would have to do something with her hair. Even though she kept her hair short, she needed to wash it every day. The tour schedule would be too tight to allow such a luxury. She decided to get a perm. She could wash her hair, run her fingers through the curls, and go.

Soon after, Debra stopped by the bank and admired Anna Joy's new hairstyle. "With all those curls, you could be Little Orphan Annie at our costume party." Debra and her housemates were planning a costume party to break the monotony of winter.

Even though parties made Anna Joy uncomfortable, she agreed to go to please her friend.

Anna Joy arrived at the party in a navy-blue dress and a red bow clipped to her curls. Cherry red rouge encircled each cheek. She sat down on the floor among a few friends, propping herself up in front of the couch. Other guests stopped by to compliment her on her new hairdo: Dorothy, Tin Man, Willie Nelson, The Singing Nun, Mary Poppins, Snow White, and the Marx Brothers. They brought her food and punch and rejoiced with her about her upcoming Israel trip.

The woman dressed as Dorothy knelt by Anna Joy, her brunette braids cascading over her shoulders. She offered Anna Joy her wicker basket. A small dog poked his head over the side, leaned toward Anna Joy, and sniffed. She slipped her hand into the basket and stroked his fluffy white coat, laughing as he licked her fingers.

"You can keep him for a while if you'd like." Dorothy smiled and went off to greet more guests, leaving "Toto" behind. Anna Joy beamed.

Next stop, *Israel*.

37.

The Promised Land

God is honored in Judah; his name is great in Israel.

Psalm 76:1 (NLT)

The items on Anna Joy's last-minute to-do list bounced around in her mind. Had she forgotten anything? She lost count of how many times she checked her watch when she was supposed to be sleeping. In a few hours, she would board a plane. Destination: Israel.

The sun had just peeked over the horizon when Allen arrived to drive her to the bus station. Anna Joy's teeth chattered in the February chill as she walked to Allen's car, dodging patches of ice. Despite the heater blowing full blast, she huddled in her seat. She was grateful she'd brought her down coat and mittens instead of the light raincoat the tour packet suggested.

Allen wheeled Anna Joy into the bus station and sat down next to her, waiting for her to board. The early morning hour did not dampen the group's excitement. Their chatter escalated in tandem with the amount of coffee consumed.

When the call sounded to board the bus, Allen wheeled Anna Joy to the door and helped her into her seat. He slipped an envelope and small package into her purse. "Don't open these until you're on the road. Have a wonderful trip." He hugged her goodbye. "I'll be praying for you."

Anna Joy pressed her nose into the windowpane and watched Allen stamp his feet and blow his frosted breath into his hands. When the bus pulled away, she placed her hand on the pane as he waved goodbye to her retreating face.

She squirmed in the seat, her legs dangling over the edge. But this was not the reason for her discomfort. She was used to her short legs not touching the floor. An uneasiness had crept over her. Even though Anna Joy had counted and recounted her money, she was still twenty dollars short. Why would God tell her to pray for a specific amount of money and then leave her twenty dollars short?

In addition to the lack of money, she didn't have any Hershey's almond bars. God always provided Hershey's almond bars as a covenant sign between them when she traveled. How could God forget? This trip was too big for God to ignore the importance of her candy bars. Maybe she wasn't supposed to go to Israel. Had she missed God?

Snatches of conversations and laughter buzzed about her. But Anna Joy stared out the window at the lingering snow. *I guess now is as good a time as any.* She reached into her purse and pulled out the envelope Allen had deposited. A Star of David stamped the seal. *Allen!* Allen had sent her all the money in the Star of David envelopes anonymously. He had promised to give her money, but she couldn't understand why she never received any funds from him.

She clutched the envelope to her chest. Allen had kept his promise. She dug in her purse for a nail file and slit open the envelope. She pulled out a twenty-dollar bill. Her last twenty dollars!

She leaned back in her seat and breathed a sigh of relief. Next, she opened the package from Allen—six Hershey's almond bars. *God, you didn't forget!* God had ordained this trip.

·~☙~·

After a fifteen-hour flight, the plane landed in Tel Aviv. Anna Joy stared at the armed soldiers stationed throughout the airport. At home, it was easy to forget that Israel lived with a constant threat of war. But she was no longer in the United States.

When the group arrived at customs, the authorities offered them the option of stamping their passport with an Israeli stamp or stamping a piece of paper. Some countries would refuse them entry if their passports bore an Israeli stamp. One by one, each member of the group requested the stamped paper, which they were instructed to keep with their passports.

The Holocaust Museum was one of their first stops on the tour. The grief and horror of the holocaust pulsated through her body with each beat of her heart as Anna Joy reflected on the brutality of the concentration camps. *How could a human being perform such atrocities on another person?* Tears spilled out of her eyes as she stifled sobs. She wanted to take time to study each photograph, each face on the wall of remembrance, and listen to their stories. But the sorrow was too great. A mausoleum of grief entombed within these walls.

Anna Joy joined the rest of the group for a tour of Jerusalem. The modern metropolis soon gave way to ancient buildings of stone and clay. She felt transported back in time, awed that she was in the land where Jesus walked, taught, and healed the sick.

They wheeled her through the crowded streets along the Via Dolorosa, following in the footsteps of Jesus to Calvary. Sorrow pierced her heart. Had his precious blood stained these cobblestone streets?

She gripped the handles of her wheelchair, jostling over the uneven streets of the old city. She had learned to trust the men in her tour group who navigated her transportation. But she didn't understand why they fought for the privilege of pushing her chair, especially when the terrain proved challenging.

As they climbed the stairs along the Via Dolorosa, the men worked together to turn her chair backward and pull her up and down the stone stairs. One grasped the handles, and the other gripped the foot pedals, steadying the chair as well as Anna Joy. They took turns pushing her as close as they could to each of the Stations of the Cross along the route.

The Via Dolorosa ended at the Church of the Holy Sepulchre, the site of Jesus's crucifixion on Golgotha. Even though the ornate church was not constructed in Jesus's time, she sensed a holy presence. She approached the slab where Nicodemus had laid Jesus's body and rested her hand on the cold stone. So close to the resurrection power of Jesus.

When they arrived at the Wailing Wall, Anna Joy's gaze followed the black-robed Orthodox Jews as they approached the wall. Their long earlocks extended from their various styles of hats and yarmulkes, denoting their sect. Some of the men had strapped phylacteries to their foreheads, containing scripture passages from the Torah.

The women wheeled Anna Joy to the women's section of the wall. Scraps of paper peeked through the crevices that breached the stones.

Anna Joy scrawled her prayer request on a slip of paper and navigated her wheelchair through the crowd of women to the wall. She stuffed her prayer request into a nearby cranny filled with other slips of paper. How many of these prayers had God answered throughout the centuries?

.౸ఴ౸.

One morning, Anna Joy shivered as she climbed onto the tour bus. This February was particularly cold. The rest of the group also huddled in their seats, blowing their breath into their hands. No amount of heat from the bus could keep them warm. She was grateful her friends had insisted she pack her down coat, down mittens, and boots.

Anna Joy's coat and mittens made the rounds of the tour group in ten-minute intervals. Even though Anna Joy shivered wearing the lightweight coats of her new friends, she was glad to share with this group of people who had taken her in and made her feel so welcome.

Despite the cold, she looked forward to a boat ride on the Sea of Galilee. She loved boats. As the choppy waves tossed the boat, she navigated her wheelchair to a place on the deck away from the brunt of the wind, and drew her fur-trimmed hood tighter around her face. She marveled that she was sailing over the sea where the disciples had fished, and where Jesus walked on the water and calmed the storm.

Anna Joy watched baptisms taking place in the Jordan River. Only a few hardy souls ventured into the frigid water. As much as she would have liked to follow Jesus's footsteps into the Jordan River and be baptized, she passed.

Groves of olive trees and the Muslim call to prayer greeted the group as they crossed into the West Bank. In Bethlehem, they joined the throngs of people entering the Church of the Nativity. Large pillars guided them through a maze of icons lining the walls of the open chamber. The purported birthplace of Jesus proved to be inaccessible. Anna Joy spent her time on the main level, studying the icons and decor while the rest of the group descended the narrow flight of stairs to the crypt.

She had saved her souvenir money for a particular purchase in Bethlehem. Their tour guide directed them to a large shop known for its plethora of olive wood nativity sets. So many to choose from. Some of the carved figurines appeared more modern, but Anna Joy preferred the traditional figures. She finally selected a beautifully carved set and arranged to have it shipped home. The shopkeeper told her the set should arrive in three months.

Occasionally, she waited on the bus during short shopping trips. But one time when the ladies returned, they each wore a dove pin carved in mother-of-pearl. Anna Joy shrank into her seat, fighting back tears. She was the only one without a dove pin. She berated herself for crying. It was just a pin.

Jericho provided a welcome warmth along with the sweetest fruit. She wiped away the juice from an orange that had dribbled down her chin. It was the best orange she'd ever tasted. She wanted to bring some oranges home, but the fruit would have been confiscated by customs officials.

At the Dead Sea, jagged cubes of salt greeted its visitors. Anna Joy would have liked to see if she could float in the mineral-rich water. She had only floated when someone held her up. But to undress and dress again would prove too time-consuming for the allotted time there.

On another day, they crossed the border into Egypt, providing them an opportunity to see the pyramids. The Egyptian guides offered horse-drawn carts for riding to the pyramids as well as camels.

One of the guides led a horse-drawn cart to Anna Joy. He bowed before her. "I have brought a cart for you to ride in, Princess."

"Oh, but I'm not a princess!" Anna Joy protested.

"Ah, but you must be a princess. No one would bring someone here in a wheelchair if they were not a princess or a very special person."

"You mean you don't see people like me in wheelchairs?"

"No, Princess. We are honored you are here. Allow me to help you into the cart." He extended his hand toward her.

Anna Joy didn't know what to say. *Princess?* "I was hoping I could ride to the pyramids on a camel."

"Of course! I'm so sorry, Princess. I'll bring the best camel for you."

He hurried away and returned a short time later with the most ornamented camel. He coaxed the camel to its knees. "Stay here at the camel's side. He can be mean. If you approach him from the front, he'll bite you and spit. Let me help you up."

He helped Anna Joy into the saddle and placed her feet in the stirrups. "Are you ready, Princess?" His face beamed. He pulled his shoulders back. He was leading the princess to the pyramids.

.⟋ᜒᜉ⟍.

As the tour drew to a close, many in her group were laden with souvenirs. Their spending budget greatly exceeded Anna Joy's. But God had one last surprise for Anna Joy. At the airport, before leaving Israel, she spotted a dove pin carved in mother-of-pearl in a little shop. Now she, too, had a dove pin to wear like all the other ladies on their tour.

When they arrived home, Anna Joy thanked the tour leader who had invited her. "I'm sorry I was so much trouble for you. You had to work so hard when this was supposed to be your vacation."

"Oh, but you don't understand." The tour leader knelt in front of Anna Joy and locked eyes with her. "This trip would not have been the same without you. We were the ones blessed by your presence. We all agree that serving you in this way was our privilege. You brought God's presence in a way we would have never experienced if you had not been with us."

Tears welled up in Anna Joy's eyes. They hadn't considered her a burden.

38.

The Carpenter Man

God has given each of you a gift from his great variety
of spiritual gifts. Use them well to serve one another.

1 Peter 4:10 (NLT)

Anna Joy's face scrunched as she navigated the stairs of the church basement to attend their weekly prayer meeting.

"You look like you're having more pain today." Scott slowed his pace as he walked alongside her.

"My mattress is too soft, and it hurts my back. I think I need a firm bed, like a captain's bed."

"I can make you one." Scott worked in his father's woodworking shop, building cabinetry.

Anna Joy paused and looked up at him. "Really? You could make me a captain's bed?"

"Sure. You just tell me what you want, and I can order the wood. We have all the equipment I need in the shop."

"I don't think I have enough money to pay for something like that."

"We can work it out. Think about what you'd like."

.⧉.

Anna Joy mentioned the possibility of a new bed to some of her friends, and they immediately agreed to pay for the bed as well as a dresser. Scott offered to donate his time.

He arrived at Anna Joy's apartment with a sketchpad and pencil. "So, how would you like your new bedroom set to look?"

"I like oak. A platform bed with drawers and a bookcase and an oak dresser."

Along with Anna Joy's input, Scott designed her ideal bedroom set. "Would you like a vanity with a mirror too?"

"That will cost a lot of money."

"Why don't you let me worry about that."

.⸙⸙.

Scott selected the oak for the furniture. He scanned the wood for knots and imperfections, selecting an attractive grain. He measured, sawed, sanded, and pounded in his spare time. One day, he invited Anna Joy into his workshop to view his progress.

She stepped across the threshold into the spacious work area and scuffed through sawdust to an area in the corner. Her eyes widened as she stared at the platform bed with two large drawers and a detached bookcase headboard. She ran her hand over the smooth oak surface. "This is beautiful."

Scott flashed her a satisfied grin. "I thought you'd like it." He flipped through a book of dresser hardware. "I've been looking for drawer pulls and found these brass ones, which I think will look nice." He showed Anna Joy the pictures, and together they made the selections.

When Scott finished the bed and dresser, he delivered them to the two-bedroom apartment where Anna Joy and her mother had recently moved. Along with a couple of friends, they took down her old bed and rearranged the furniture in her bedroom to make space for the new. They placed Anna Joy's new, very firm mattress on the captain's bed. "Why don't you try it out?"

With the help of her crutches, Anna Joy pushed herself up onto the mattress and lay down on her back. "This is perfect!"

"I made hand pulls here to help you get out of bed." Scott showed her where he had placed the handles.

"You thought of everything!"

Her friends helped her make the bed and organize her clothes in the new drawers.

.⸙.

When Scott finished the vanity, he delivered it to Anna Joy's home.

She marveled at the craftsmanship. She never anticipated such a magnificent piece of furniture. Three drawers lined either side of the vanity, leaving room for a chair in the middle. The mirror was comprised of three hinged sections that adjusted for multiple viewing angles. "It's gorgeous."

Scott pulled up a chair. "Here. Sit down, and I'll show you how everything works." He adjusted the mirrors at various angles and opened the drawers for her.

"What are those compartments beneath the mirrors?"

"I know how much you like jewelry, so I built jewelry compartments for you." Scott opened two long, shallow drawers at the back of the vanity. "These drawers will hold your necklaces." He lifted the lid of another compartment. "You can store smaller items in here, like your brooches." Next, he reached toward the back of a compartment and pulled the lid forward, revealing rows of velvet-lined grooves. "Your rings will slip into these compartments."

Anna Joy gasped.

"I knew you would like this." Scott grinned. "It took me a while to figure out how to make it."

After Scott left, Anna Joy thanked God for her furniture. "Lord, you are the master builder. I know Scott was an instrument in your hands, and you inspired him to create this incredible bedroom set just for me."

Anna Joy asked her friends to hang two of her favorite pencil drawings of Jesus on her wall above the vanity. The first picture featured Jesus as a child clothed in a robe with a rope tied around his waist. One hand raised a mallet while the other hand steadied a chisel, gouging a piece of wood. The second picture portrayed an adult Jesus sanding a block of wood.

Several years later, Scott introduced her to a song about Jesus, the carpenter man. This song, along with the pictures, reflected the Jesus she knew and loved. Jesus, who twirled her around, carried her on his shoulders, and laughed with joy. He was the carpenter man, who inspired her bedroom set.

39.

Sand and Surf

The LORD has done great things for us, and we are filled with joy.

Psalm 126:3 (NIV)

Derek and Catherine hugged Anna Joy at the airport. "We can't believe you're actually here!" They chimed in unison, "We've missed you!" They had invited Anna Joy, their spiritual mother, to visit them in St Petersburg, Florida, where Derek was temporarily assigned with the navy.

"I can hardly believe I'm here either!" As they exited the terminal, the stifling heat and humidity blasted Anna Joy's face. She paused and drew in a deep breath.

"What would you like to do while you're here?" Catherine stayed with her while Derek fetched the car.

"Can we go to the beach?"

"Absolutely!"

That evening after dinner, they caught up on the events of the past few months.

"Our wedding pictures came. Do you want to see them?" Derek didn't wait for an answer. He brought the pictures to Anna Joy. "My brothers were so mad after our wedding." Derek threw his head back and chortled.

Anna Joy laughed too as she remembered that day six months prior.

As the reception had drawn to a close, Derek beckoned Anna Joy into an empty back hallway. He knelt on one knee in front of her wheelchair. "I have a big favor to ask you. When my brother got married a few months ago, my family trashed his car and placed the vehicle on blocks so he couldn't drive away. I'm afraid they'll try to hamper our getaway or follow us to the hotel and serenade us with a raucous shivaree. Since they don't know where we're staying, I need to sneak out without my brothers seeing me. Will you be my decoy?"

"Of course! I'll take every extra minute I can get with you!"

"Catherine snuck away to change. She will meet me in the parking ramp where I hid the car." Derek glanced down the long, dark hallway. A shadowy figure resembling one of his brothers disappeared around the corner. Derek chuckled as he glanced down the hall. "I'm hoping they'll get bored waiting for me to leave so I can get away. My brothers don't understand why I'd spend so much time with a woman in a wheelchair who's not family."

Occasionally one of Derek's brothers poked his head around the corner and then disappeared.

After some time passed, Derek's brother reappeared in the hallway. Too late. Derek had escaped with his bride.

Anna Joy sat in her wheelchair and smiled sweetly at him. Their ruse had worked.

.⸙.

Each day after Derek left for the base, Catherine sat on the floor with Anna Joy. They talked and prayed together. Just as Anna Joy had learned how to pray at her grandmother's knees, she taught Catherine. Each day was filled with hours of prayer accompanied by weeping as Catherine moved into new levels of intercession.

When the weekend arrived, Derek said, "Are we still on for the beach tomorrow?"

Anna Joy could hardly contain her excitement.

After unpacking the car the next morning, Derek maneuvered her wheelchair through the sand and seashell fragments. The wheels got stuck in ruts, requiring him to repeatedly back up before he could push her forward again. Dry sand gave way to wet, squishy sand, stalling their progress. "I didn't remember it being this far. I hope you're doing okay."

Finally, they reached the shoreline. A pungent odor, mingled with sea air, wafted past their nostrils as the waves lapped over the sand.

"Put me in the water."

Derek pushed the wheelchair into the murky waters until the ripples tickled over her toes.

She kicked her feet as best as she could. "Push me in more!"

Derek held on to the handles of the chair and pushed her in until the waves brushed her knees.

Catherine stationed herself in the surf off to the side and in front of Anna Joy. She laughed as Anna Joy squealed in delight.

"Push me in further!"

Derek locked eyes with Catherine. "I don't know if we should go in much further."

"I want to go in deeper!"

Derek shook his head. "Okay, here we go." He gripped the handles and pushed her wheelchair further into the water, steadying the chair with each crash of the waves.

Anna Joy bounced up and down in her chair as the foamy waters smacked her chest.

Catherine braced herself near the front of the chair. "I hope these waves don't toss you out into the sea. It's a good thing I spent so many summers working as a lifeguard."

When the time came to leave, Derek backed Anna Joy's wheelchair out of the water while Catherine helped steady her from the front. Together they tugged and pulled the wheelchair up an incline, through the ruts and sand until they reached the parking lot.

Derek inspected the wheelchair. "I don't think this wheelchair was meant to be subjected to all this sand and salt."

When they got back to the house, Derek pulled the wheelchair apart, piece by piece. He rinsed each part with the hose. Sand had clogged every nook and cranny. "I think I got all the sand out. Now I hope it doesn't rust."

As the evening progressed, a pink hue, courtesy of the sun, spread and deepened over Anna Joy's skin. But she didn't care if she was sunburned. She had frolicked in the sea.

40.

A Birthday Blessing

O LORD my God, I cried out to You, And You healed me.

Psalm 30:2 (NKJV)

Anna Joy grasped the rail at the top of the staircase leading from her apartment to the ground floor, and in her typical fashion, tossed one of her crutches down the steps. She preferred to manage the descent unencumbered by the second crutch. The crutch bounced and clattered until it landed on the floor below. She began to descend, but after several steps, her heel caught on the edge of the previous stair. She teetered, lost her balance, and tumbled the rest of the way down.

Once again, she found herself sprawled on the floor, choking on dust stirred up by her fall. Catching her breath, she raised up on her hands and knees. *Where are my glasses?* She spotted them nearby and slipped them over her nose. No damage there.

She grabbed the rail, pulled her body around, and seated herself on the lowest step. She reviewed each body part, checking for injuries. She seemed to have survived this fall unscathed. Mentally, she again thanked the physical therapists who spent hours teaching her how to fall so as to avoid serious injury.

Anna Joy brushed the dirt from her skirt. Her bus would be along shortly, and she couldn't afford to be late for work. She picked up her crutches and walked toward the bus stop. Each time she exerted pressure on one of her crutches, stabbing pain shot through her shoulder. She winced. Hopefully this discomfort would be temporary.

.⁓☙⁓.

Months passed, and Anna Joy's shoulder still throbbed, especially when she walked. She also couldn't get comfortable lying on that shoulder at night. She prayed for healing and enlisted healing prayers from her friends. Seemingly to no avail.

One day, Anna Joy received a long-distance phone call, a rarity since these calls were so expensive.

"Ruby? How are you? It's been so long. I've missed you!"

Ruby chuckled. "I've missed you too! I'm calling because the Lord told me to come for your birthday and pray for your shoulder."

Anna Joy's mouth dropped open. But no words spilled out.

"Anna Joy? Are you still there?"

"Yes! How did you know I hurt my shoulder? I never told you!" She had always valued Ruby's intercession.

Ruby chuckled. "Never underestimate God!"

"You're really coming? I can't wait to see you! You'll be my best birthday present!"

"Good! I'll call you later with my flight information."

Anna Joy grinned, barely able to contain the good news. Ruby was coming!

.⁓☙⁓.

Anna Joy arranged for Allen to take her to the airport and pick up Ruby. Her heart raced as she hopped into his car, rejoicing that God had sent Ruby for her birthday.

Anna Joy's crutches pounded the airport linoleum as she searched for her friend. *There she is!*

Ruby peered over the glasses perched on her nose beneath waves of white hair streaked with shades of gray. The corners of her mouth curved to form a wide grin. Ruby reached for her wooden crutches, slipped off the chair, and pulled herself up to all of her nearly four-foot height. She made a beeline toward Anna Joy, embracing her in a hug. After introductions, she followed Allen and Anna Joy to the car.

Anna Joy's friends had planned a dinner to celebrate her birthday and welcome Ruby. But before the party, Ruby pulled Anna Joy aside. "The Lord sent me here to pray for your shoulder, and that's what I'm going to do." Ruby prayed, asking God to heal Anna Joy's shoulder.

After Ruby prayed, Anna Joy moved her shoulder around. "My shoulder doesn't hurt! God answered your prayer. He healed my shoulder! Thank you for praying, Ruby!"

Every year, Anna Joy waited for the special birthday gift God had promised he would give her. Year after year, his promise never failed. This year, that gift came wrapped as a healing prayer through the hands of her dear friend and intercessor, Ruby.

Anna Joy beamed when she arrived at her birthday dinner. She couldn't wait to introduce her friends to Ruby and share the good news about God's healing power. Her friends gathered around the large dining room table, welcomed Ruby, and celebrated Anna Joy's healing. They also celebrated the gift Anna Joy was to them with cake, presents, and words of encouragement.

When the time arrived for Ruby to fly home, she hugged Anna Joy goodbye with tears in her eyes. "You're like a daughter to me. You've made some good friends here, Anna Joy. I know I'm leaving you in good hands."

Later, Anna Joy wondered if Ruby had known this would be the last time they would see each other.

41.

Doctor, Doctor

She had suffered a great deal from many doctors, and over the years she had spent everything she had to pay them, but she had gotten no better. In fact, she had gotten worse.

Mark 5:26 (NLT)

"Throw those pills away." Scott took the bottle of pills out of Anna Joy's hand. "They're making you sick."

"But I haven't had any bladder accidents since I started taking them." Anna joy wheezed out the words between coughing jags. "I don't have to go to the bathroom as often."

"Look at you! You can hardly breathe because your lungs are so full of fluid. Your legs look like swollen sausages." Scott pressed his finger into her calf. "See? My finger leaves an indentation an inch deep. That's called pitting edema."

"I looked up this medicine, and it's contraindicated for kidney disease. Your doctor should have known this. Maybe it's time you get a new doctor." Scott waved the pill bottle.

Anna Joy fought to catch her breath but finally acquiesced. Scott was right. "I won't take them anymore." But it had been so nice not to be wet all the time.

.⸙.

Anna Joy decided to try another doctor recommended by a friend. She didn't like doctors. Their tests always hurt. She wasn't sure she wanted to see this one because he specialized in kidney disease.

The new doctor talked with her about her previous medical history and concerns. She showed him the bottle of pills the other doctor had prescribed for her bladder accidents.

He looked at the bottle, shook his head, and threw it in the wastebasket. "That doctor has problems." He began his head-to-toe examination. After listening to her lungs, he slung the stethoscope around his neck. "I can hear the fluid crackling in your lungs. How's your breathing?"

"Sometimes it's hard to breathe when I'm walking, but I do okay." She forced a smile.

The doctor bent over and pressed on her calves, leaving his finger mark indentations. "You have three-plus pitting edema. Are your legs always swollen like this?" He peered into Anna Joy's face.

She looked down at her hands. "Sometimes. It's worse at the end of the day."

"You must be in a lot of pain." The doctor sat back in his chair. "I'm going to tell you what you should do. And you're going to tell me what you will do."

Anna Joy didn't know what to say. No doctor had ever negotiated with her before. They usually demanded absolute obedience to their orders.

"I'm going to give you some information to think about. We'll schedule another appointment to talk about a plan that you can live with." He handed her several brochures before she left the office.

"I really like that doctor," Anna Joy told Debra.

Several months later, Debra showed her a newspaper clipping about her new doctor. He had lost his life in a small plane crash. He was thirty-five years old.

Anna Joy groaned. She would never have a chance to see him for that follow-up appointment. He had been a good doctor.

.⚬ℒℯ⚬.

Anna Joy pressed her hand to her ear and sobbed. Another sharp pain shot through her ear. It had been a long time since she had suffered from an ear infection this bad. Her mom dripped some sweet oil drops in her ear, just as she had done many times in the past. But her ear still throbbed.

That evening a friend called to check on Anna Joy. "I think we need to take you to the emergency room."

"I'll be fine." Anna Joy sniffed. "It's not my first ear infection." She cried out as another wave of pain stabbed her eardrum.

"I'm going to come get you."

Anna Joy arrived in the emergency room, and she and her friend were taken back into a cubicle.

"The doctor will be with you shortly." The nurse pulled the curtain around them.

As her friend tried to make her comfortable, a doctor was paged over the PA system.

"This is a hospital!" Anna Joy pulled herself upright on the cart. "I hate hospitals! I want to go home now!"

"You haven't seen the doctor yet." Her friend helped her lie back down on the cart.

"You didn't tell me you were taking me to a hospital! I would've never come! I want to go home."

The doctor pulled back the curtain. "I heard we have someone here who doesn't like hospitals. Who hurt you so bad that you don't like us? I promise I won't hurt you. Will you let me look at your ears now? If it hurts, I'll stop."

Anna Joy watched him warily, her nod barely perceptible.

The doctor picked up the otoscope, gently held her outer ear, and slipped the scope into her ear canal. He looked toward Anna Joy as if to gauge her reaction. He pulled the scope back when she winced. "We're done. You have three different types of ear infections.

It's a good thing you came in when you did. You risked hearing loss. I'm going to prescribe some ear drops for you: a steroid, an antibiotic, and a pain killer. You should feel better soon."

"Will you be here if I have to come back?" She could hope.

"No, I'm almost done with my residency, and then I will be moving back East." He smiled.

After he left, Anna Joy wiped away the tears. "He's really nice, for a doctor. I wish he could be my doctor."

.ᴗଓଡ଼ᴗ.

Anna Joy scheduled a visit with a different doctor recommended by a friend. After giving her a thorough examination, he sat back in his chair. "You have quite a few medical issues we need to follow up on. I'm going to order some lab tests. I'll refer you to a urologist to place a scope in your bladder and ureters. We'll probably need to do a renal scan as well." The doctor started writing out his orders.

"I already had all those tests done." Anna Joy felt her body tense. "They told me there was nothing they could do to help me. I can't see the point in doing them again." No way was she going to let them do those awful tests again and then tell her it was all for nothing.

"I think the tests are important. The results might be different now. We really need to know what's going on today."

"I'm sorry. I can't go through those tests again. Last time it took me weeks to recover from the pain. Besides, needles literally bounce off my skin. No one can get an IV in my veins or even draw my blood."

"I think we need to do these tests, so we know what's going on."

"I can't do them again."

"If you're not going to do what I recommend, then I guess there's no reason for you to come back to my office." He got up from his desk and strode out of the exam room without a backward glance.

Anna Joy picked up her crutches and walked out of the clinic. She had made her decision—no more doctors.

42.

A Christmas Miracle

He hears the prayers of the righteous.

Proverbs 15:29 (NLT)

Anna Joy shivered as she sat in her recliner with blankets piled on top of her. She hoped her body temperature wouldn't rise to the febrile levels it had when she was a child and experienced fever-induced seizures. Another coughing fit convulsed her body. She gasped for breath. Pain seized her chest and radiated throughout her back and rib cage. She figured she had another bout of pneumonia. But this time was different. She didn't think her body could hold out much longer.

The doorbell pulled her mind back to her friend Debra. She had told Anna Joy she would stop by before heading home for Christmas. Anna Joy was grateful her mother was home to answer the door. The last thing she wanted to do was come out from under the comfort and warmth of her blankets. As her mother walked by, Anna Joy caught a faint whiff of her favorite chicken dumpling soup simmering on the stove.

Debra hugged her friend. Her brow furrowed as she studied her. "You're not looking so good."

Anna Joy squirmed under Debra's scrutiny. She didn't want Debra the nurse. She wanted Debra her friend. She tried to rally a smile. "I'll get better. I've had pneumonia before." She attempted to sound chipper, but another coughing jag snagged her voice.

As Debra prayed for her, Anna Joy could hear the worry in her tone. She recognized the fear in Debra's eyes.

After Debra left, Anna Joy prayed. "Lord, please be with Debra as she travels home, and calm her fears. And Lord, she won't understand if you decide to take me home while she is away."

Since many of Anna Joy's friends were students, they, along with Debra, would be out of town with their families for Christmas. Maybe a few of her friends in the area would stop by and pray for her.

Aaron and his wife, Miriam, had written that they would be in the area visiting family and friends over Christmas break. They had been members of the prayer group and considered her their spiritual mother. But once Aaron completed his doctoral studies, he accepted a university professorship, and they moved out East.

Anna Joy sensed the Lord telling her, "If Aaron comes and prays for you, I will heal you. But you can't ask him. He must come of his own accord. You must understand; if he prays for you, I will heal you, but your life will be very difficult. You will experience great pain. You will suffer much."

Anna Joy didn't expect Aaron to come. He was in town for a short time and would probably be too busy with family and friends to sense a nudge from the Lord to come and pray for her.

"Lord, I need a Christmas miracle."

.·ᴥ⊛ᴥ·.

Anna Joy closed her eyes, hoping her body would allow her to catch a little sleep. She tried to rest in her recliner to ease the wheezing, but another coughing spell wracked her body. She glanced at the clock and pulled the blanket tighter around her neck. She wasn't sure how much longer she would survive.

The doorbell jarred her attempts to sleep.

When her mom opened the door, Aaron strode toward Anna Joy. "The Lord told me to come and pray for you." He laid his hands on her head. "Oh my! God, . . ." Aaron prayed for healing. Then he bolted out the door.

As the Christmas season progressed, Anna Joy's cough and wheezing eased, and her fever abated. She knew she would recover. The Lord was faithful. Aaron had listened to God and prayed.

Later Aaron revealed to Anna Joy what he had seen when he prayed. "I saw a picture of your lungs struggling to breathe, blackened, and filled with infection. I was so scared. I didn't know how to pray for you."

Anna Joy smiled. "But God knew. You came and he answered your prayer."

43.

Born to Pray

The earnest prayer of a righteous person has great
power and produces wonderful results.

James 5:16 (NLT)

"I was born to pray." Anna Joy chuckled. "I think intercession must be embedded in my DNA. Prayer is not dull or boring. Praying for others is part of loving them as Jesus loves them. When we pray, we partner with God to bring about his will in our lives, like in the Our Father. 'Thy will be done on earth as it is in heaven' (Matthew 6:10).

"I start by asking the Holy Spirit how he wants me to pray. I listen to God with one ear, and I listen to the person with the other ear, so I know how to pray. He may give me a Scripture for that person, a specific word, or a picture to help bring clarity to their situation. Sometimes I know how to pray for a person because I feel pain in a certain part of my body. When I experience what they're feeling, I know how to pray for them. I may feel overwhelmed by a negative emotion for no reason, like depression, fear, or anxiety. Later that person might come back to me and tell me the oppression has lifted."

Anna Joy answered the cries of the hurting, whether day or night. She developed a reputation throughout the city for helping people recover from traumas, abuse, and life's hurts. She was a lifeline for many people in crisis situations and prayed for them over the phone, day or night, as well as scheduled times for prayer.

She counseled from the one book that had brought her healing and deliverance. The Bible. Anna Joy delighted in the Word of God. She often thumbed through her Bible with its ragged edges, marked pages, and highlighted passages. If she didn't know where a specific Scripture was located, the Lord would tell her where to find the verse or passage she needed. He would lead her to specific Scriptures that would bring freedom to the people she prayed with. She reminded them that the Word of God was as relevant today as it was when it was first written.

Anna Joy often befriended the people the Lord directed her to pray for. One time she noticed the next-door neighbor of a friend lumber across his backyard toward his large pigeon enclosure. He was a quiet, middle-aged man who cared for his mother. She heard in her spirit, *He's a very lonely man. I want you to be his friend.* She asked God how to connect with him. *Ask him about his pigeons.* She didn't know anything about pigeons, nor was she particularly interested in pigeons, but she obeyed the Lord's instructions.

"You have a lot of pigeons over there. I don't know anything about pigeons. What do you do with them?"

He gave her a quizzical look. "They're homing pigeons. Come on over, and I'll introduce you." He beamed as he told her about each of the birds, how he cared for them and trained them. As he gently handled a bird, removing one from the enclosure, the pigeon cooed. He held it out so Anna Joy could stroke his head.

Whenever Anna Joy visited her friend, she would visit the man and his birds. He also cultivated the most beautiful peonies. When he found out peonies were one of Anna Joy's favorite flowers, he created gorgeous bouquets for her to take home.

.ᦔᦉᦆ.

One day she looked out her window and thought she saw her friend walking down the sidewalk in her brightly colored poncho. *Lord, that can't be her. She's at work.* She sensed the Lord wanted her to pray for her friend, so she prayed.

Later her friend told her that during the time Anna Joy was praying, she was sitting at the bedside of a young man who was dying. "I felt like his spirit was hovering between heaven and hell. Where he would spend eternity was in the balance. I don't know what he chose, but I was praying he would choose Jesus. You must have been praying for him too."

.⁓⁓.

Another time, Anna Joy picked up the phone. A familiar voice on the other end of the line choked back sobs. "The doctor just told me I have metastatic breast cancer. I've been to so many doctors in the past few months because of back pain, and now they're telling me that the pain in my back is due to bone metastasis. I'm five months pregnant, and I don't know what to do. The doctor wants me to have an abortion. I won't kill my baby."

"I'll be right there."

Anna Joy prayed. *Lord, I need you to tell me how to pray for my friend. I want you to heal her, but I want to pray how you want me to pray.*

After much prayer, she sensed the Lord telling her not to pray for her friend's healing because he was not going to heal her. "I want you to pray for a healthy baby and that her pelvis will carry the pregnancy. The cancer has eaten holes in her pelvic bone."

This was not the news Anna Joy hoped to hear, but she prayed as the Lord directed. She asked the doctor if the woman's "moth-eaten" pelvis could support the baby. The doctor whirled toward her. "How do you know what her pelvis looks like? Have you seen the x-ray?" She had not.

Anna Joy prayed her friend through the pregnancy and through the side effects of a chemotherapy drug the doctor said shouldn't affect the baby. One day Anna Joy received a call. "We have a healthy, five-pound baby boy."

God had answered her prayers.

.⟶₰₰⟶.

Anna Joy loved praying for babies. When a friend told her she was pregnant, Anna Joy sensed that the baby was at risk. She prayed for a safe delivery and healthy baby. But this baby was different. Each week she laid her hand on the mama's belly and prayed. The cadence of her voice would change. It was as if she carried on a joy-filled conversation with the baby.

The parents invited her to be present at the birth. When the father placed the baby in her arms, she sensed that God had special plans for this baby girl. She would carry a powerful anointing to bring about justice. No wonder the Lord had called Anna Joy to pray for this little one. The Enemy had targeted the little one from the womb.

.⟶₰₰⟶.

Anna Joy became known as a birthing intercessor. "Birthing doesn't just happen in the physical. But birthing occurs in the Spirit," she said. She quoted Jesus's words to Nicodemus: "Humans can reproduce only human life, but the Holy Spirit gives birth to spiritual life. So don't be surprised when I say, 'You must be born again'" (John 3:6–7 NLT).

"Sometimes in intercession, you feel like you're giving birth," Anna Joy said. "You may be birthing something in the Spirit. Maybe someone is coming to know Jesus. Maybe it's a new ministry, or a new move of God. You may groan and feel like your pelvis is being pulled apart. I often experience this when I'm praying for someone to know Jesus. I told the Lord that I sometimes feel like a broodmare!"

Anna Joy's letters were often filled with words of counsel and prayer.

She wrote to a friend:

No reason to write except that you've been on my mind, and I just wanted to remind you that you are loved by both the Lord and me. For some reason, I feel you need this reminder right now. I also have been praying for you.

God has been so good to me, blessing me with his presence and his Word. I have learned much about myself, good and bad, and what God wants from me. Despite what I've seen about myself that's negative, I am filled with hope and confidence even in my present circumstances. That's the God I know. He can accomplish anything in anybody. And because he is in me, I can accomplish anything that he wishes me to do. But I have never experienced such warfare to get me to believe the opposite. God must be up to something good.

Your letter was full of good news, and a welcome addition to my mailbox. "Like cold water to a weary soul is good news from a distant land" (Proverbs 25:25 NIV).

It has been a heavy week of counseling. Depression and despair seem rampant. Spiritual warfare virulent. Could it be due to my continuing study and teaching on the subject? It was good so I could get my mind off my own problems.

You ask how I handle my own pain. I pray, telling God exactly how I feel. I reach out to help others, and I occasionally talk to certain people about it: my spiritual director, or a close friend if God leads and they are available. I also praise God for who he is, and what he has already done.

"Do not be anxious about anything, but in every situation, by prayer and petition, with thanksgiving, present your requests to God. And the peace of God, which transcends all understanding, will guard your hearts and your minds in Christ Jesus. Finally, brothers and sisters, whatever is true, whatever is noble, whatever is right, whatever is pure, whatever is lovely, whatever is admirable—if anything is excellent or praiseworthy—think about such things" (Philippians 4:6-8 NIV).

44.

Prayer Group Family

*How good and pleasant it is when God's
people live together in unity!*

Psalm 133:1 (NIV)

Anna Joy belted out the lively song at the close of the prayer meeting. She watched as some of the prayer group members joined hands and danced around the room. Suddenly she felt her wheelchair jerk. Hands had reached around and unlocked her wheelchair.

Debra smiled and pulled Anna Joy's wheelchair out of the circle and spun her around the room, trailing the dancers.

Anna Joy clapped and sang along with the group. No matter what event they attended, someone would invariably grasp her wheelchair and pull her into the dancing. They made her forget her disability. Sometimes she even led the line of dancers.

When the song and the encore ended, a red-faced Debra returned Anna Joy to the circle and disappeared into the crowd.

Anna Joy waited, knowing that before long, someone would approach her for counseling or prayer. It hadn't taken long for the members of the group to recognize her ability to hear God, impart words of wisdom, and pray for their current situations.

As the crowd cleared, Debra collected the songbooks and packed them away while Allen stacked the chairs. They would return for Anna Joy when it was time to leave.

The last person who sought her out that evening thanked her and hugged her goodbye. Anna Joy snapped her compact Bible shut and slipped it back into her purse. While she checked the floor around her for any stray belongings, a burly man approached her. As he brushed up against her, she stiffened. Without looking up, she knew he was one of the street people who occasionally dropped in during the prayer meetings. But none of the street people terrified her as much as this man.

Allen glanced over toward Anna Joy. He dropped the chair that he was about to stack and dashed toward her. Without a word, he slid his body between the man, nearly twice his size, and Anna Joy.

The man's eyes widened. He backed away and hurried out the door.

"Are you okay?" Allen helped her into her coat.

Anna Joy nodded, grateful Allen seemed to have appointed himself as her unofficial protector and bouncer. She figured the man must not have noticed Allen. The word on the street was that he was terrified of Allen. If she weren't so frightened, she'd be amused because Allen had such a quiet and gentle spirit.

After Allen finished stacking the few remaining chairs, he took hold of the wheelchair, pulled her up the stairs, and out to Debra's car.

Since the beginning of their friendship, Debra had given her rides to and from the prayer meetings. Each week, Debra picked her up after work at the bank and then drove to their favorite Italian restaurant. After a spaghetti dinner, they headed to the prayer meeting.

.ৎ৯৯৬.

One evening after the prayer meeting, one of the leaders sat down next to Anna Joy. "The leadership team has been praying about adding new leaders to our team. We feel that God may be calling you to lead."

Anna Joy squirmed in her chair. She hoped she wasn't hearing right. But God had been speaking to her about leadership. She knew that bringing in new leaders was one of the frustrations that plagued the leadership team. More than once, the team recognized God raising up a leader, but all too soon, that leader graduated and moved away. The university town was a revolving door of hellos and goodbyes.

"We've watched how God has used you since you've been here. The words you have spoken from the Lord during our meetings have been right on. We know how much you have helped our members by counseling and praying with them. As leaders, we need your wisdom as we seek the Lord and his direction for our group."

"I'll pray about it." Anna Joy muttered as she looked down at her trembling hands.

On the way home, she told Debra about their request.

"That's awesome! You'd be perfect!"

Debra's enthusiasm didn't surprise her, but Anna Joy wasn't thrilled about being on the leadership team. Leadership always came with a price tag. The last thing she wanted was the Enemy to pin a target on her back.

As Anna Joy prayed, she knew the Lord was calling her to join that core group for this young group of believers. She joined the team of five others, including Allen, Benny and his wife, and another couple. They met weekly for dinner, prayer, and leadership business.

While serving on the leadership team, Anna Joy helped to oversee the Life in the Spirit Seminars, a seven-week program consisting of talks and small groups designed to lead people into a deeper relationship with the Holy Spirit. She also helped develop a spiritual growth seminar that included teachings and weekly small group meetings. As an intercessor, she prayed for the other leaders as well as the members under her spiritual care.

.ఎఠు.

The leaders sensed the Lord calling them to explore Christian community. The prayer group already experienced many aspects of community life. They not only prayed together but played together. They camped, canoed, sledded, and took dance lessons. They hosted potlucks and parties, celebrated birthdays and weddings, planned retreats and attended Christian conferences together. In many ways, the group had become an extended family.

What would Christian community look like? They studied other models of community and visited with their leaders. Did community living mean families and singles living together? Were they called to live in close proximity to one another so they could be more involved in one another's lives on a daily basis? As leaders, they explored these and other questions with the group's committed members.

.ఎఠు.

One summer, the leadership team decided to take a vacation together. It would be an opportunity to build relationships with one another and experience community for a week. The team, plus four children under five, rented a cottage on a lake, about four hours away.

Anna Joy walked into the cottage and scanned the large wood-paneled room with its ample table and long hallway leading to the four bedrooms. The kitchen was fully equipped and should be able to meet their needs. This could be an interesting weekend.

A steady rain fell as morning dawned on the first day of vacation. With all outdoor activities tabled, entertaining four little ones proved challenging. The next day, a downpour muddied the ground. The continual drizzle not only dampened their spirits but sent a chill into their bones. So much for warm weather and fun in the sun.

By the third day, the sun peaked through the clouds. When the cottage owner offered them the use of his pontoon boat, they jumped at the chance to be out on the water. They strapped the children into life jackets and boarded the vessel.

Allen maneuvered Anna Joy's wheelchair onto the boat beneath the edge of the canopy and locked her wheels. She loved boat rides, whether pontoon, sailboats, or speedboats.

A gentle breeze ruffled the canopy as they motored away from the pier with Benny initially at the helm. Even though the sun warmed her face, Anna Joy pulled her sweatshirt tighter around her neck. She didn't care if she felt chilled from the occasional gusts of wind. She was sailing over the gentle waves. She watched a couple of others try their hands at the wheel before the afternoon outing ended.

The next day they visited a deer farm and petting zoo. In the goat pen, Allen chased down a baby goat for her to hold. The goat seemed more interested in exploring Anna Joy's jacket and munching on her collar. Other goats flocked around Anna Joy. But they weren't only drawn to the food she held in her hand. They sniffed her wheelchair tires and attempted to nibble on her leather purse as well as the leather covering of her forearm crutches.

"We'd better get you out of here before they do any damage." Allen pushed the wheelchair out of the pen where she could feed the goats from a safe distance—through the fence.

In the meantime, she heard the boys tearing through the geese pen, chasing the flock. They stirred up a ruckus as well as a flurry of feathers.

Soon the boys joined Anna Joy and Allen at the fence. Little fists wrapped around the goat food. The goats moseyed over and flocked around them. Giggles erupted from the boys as the critters nibbled the food from their hands through the fencing.

Corn dispensers to feed the deer dotted another area of the farm. Allen took a handful of corn and poured some into Anna Joy's hand. A deer boldly approached her and greedily nuzzled her hand. Anna Joy patted his nose and stroked his soft antlers. But the buck seemed to lose interest in her once the corn disappeared.

The week ended on a celebratory note with a birthday party for the five-year-old.

.⁓ஃஃ⁓.

The leadership team had been together for several years when the two wives spoke up at their weekly meeting. "We feel that it's time to leave the team and the prayer group. It's become too much with raising young children," one said.

Anna Joy pursed her lips, saddened by this announcement. Even though this news wasn't totally unexpected, she grieved the loss of weekly fellowship with the other women on the team, who had become her close friends.

Many months later, the two husbands approached Allen and Anna Joy. "We decided it's time to step down from the leadership team and the prayer group."

One of the leaders continued, "Our oldest is starting school this fall, and we get home from the meetings too late for him to go to bed on time."

Anna Joy knew the prayer meetings lasted too late in the evening for these families. Already, the wives stayed home to attend to the needs of the children. She and Allen stayed late after the meetings to be sure the room was put back in order so those leaders with families could leave.

With both couples leaving the team, she sensed the time had come for her to depart as well. They weren't just a team. They were a unit. She had forged deep friendships with each member of the team.

Her heart broke. Her dream of Christian community within the prayer group died.

45.

The Legacy of Two Grandmothers

Be merciful to those who doubt; save others
by snatching them from the fire.

Jude 22-23 (NIV)

Anna Joy scurried toward the jangling phone, hoping she wouldn't miss an important call. "Hello?" Her chest heaved as she struggled to catch her breath. She heard the voice of a close relative on the other end of the line.

"Your Grandma Wilma's dying. It's cancer," he said. "If you want to see her, you'd better get down there. Your dad's with her now."

Anna Joy phoned her friend Benny. "My grandma's dying. Can you take me to see her?" She did not want to face her dad alone. She knew he resented her for taking his wife, her mother, away from him. Since her visit to California, her few interactions with her father had been at family gatherings where she felt either ridiculed or ignored by him—though she couldn't decide which hurt more. But she knew her dad would be less likely to reveal his contempt if she brought a male friend. "It'll be my last chance to share Jesus with her." She paused. "My dad will be there."

⋅◦§◦⋅

Anna Joy stared out the window as Benny drove the six hours to Grandma Wilma's house. She recalled the last time she'd received a call to come home.

She had carved out a few moments from her busy schedule to listen to the stereo with her kitty, purring in her lap. The jingle of the phone had interrupted her solitude.

"Your Grandma Grace had a stroke." Mom's voice cracked. "She's in the hospital and hasn't woken up."

"I'll get home as soon as I can."

Anna Joy had prayed, "Please, God, help me get home in time. And God, can you provide money for a ticket too?"

Anna Joy scrambled to pack a bag. She knew she had a long flight ahead of her. A knock on the door had interrupted her packing. A woman from her church stood in the doorway.

She handed Anna Joy an envelope. "The Lord told me to give this to you." She turned and walked away.

"Thank you!" Anna Joy said to the retreating form. She opened the envelope and counted the twenty-dollar bills. Enough to pay her plane fare. "Thank you, Jesus!" she'd prayed.

.ᴼᵉ⌐.

Tap, tap. Anna Joy remembered now how her crutches had echoed down the corridors of the hospital. She could almost smell the all-too-familiar antiseptic odors mingled with the stench of body fluids. She'd scrunched her nose. She eyed the numbers on the doors until reaching the partially opened door matching the slip of paper given to her at the information desk.

"Anna Joy!" Auntie had hugged her and then directed Anna Joy to a chair next to Grandma's bed. "She hasn't woken up at all." Auntie sat down on the other side of the bed. "Your mom will be coming soon."

Grandma's gray hair had been arranged in her usual bun. Several white pillows supported her head, nearly matching the pallor of her face. Each snoring breath sucked her cheeks against her gums. Grandma didn't like anyone to see her without her teeth.

Anna Joy reached under the covers and grasped Grandma's hand. "Hi, Grandma. It's me. Anna Joy."

Grandma had opened her eyes.

"She hasn't responded to any of us all week, not even her own children." Auntie pressed her lips together in a thin, hard line. "Except you. You always were her favorite."

Tears rolled down Anna Joy's cheeks and plopped onto Grandma's hand as she said goodbye to the grandma who had faithfully prayed for her all these years. A grandma who had taught her how to pray, taught her to believe in Jesus, and taught her to believe in miracles.

Now, she was on her way to another goodbye.

·⌒o⚬o⌒·

Screams from inside the house greeted Anna Joy and Benny upon their arrival to this summons to her paternal grandmother's bedside.

"She's dying," her dad said. "I'm giving her as much morphine as the doctor lets me, but no matter how much I give her, it only keeps her quiet for a short time."

Anna Joy sat at her grandmother's bedside, holding her hand, singing, and reading Scripture to her—Psalm 23, Psalm 91, and John 14. When Grandma woke, she'd tell her about Jesus.

When Anna Joy began speaking, Grandma's lucidity only lasted a few moments before she started to thrash again. Grandma glared at Anna Joy. "I don't need your Jesus!"

"But you're dying, Grandma. Don't you want to go to heaven and be with Jesus?"

"No! I'd rather go to hell!" Grandma grimaced and cried out.

Anna Joy's dad ran in and grabbed the morphine. "I got another shot for you, Mom."

Benny sat with Grandma and shared about Jesus—until she demanded he leave.

Anna Joy knew the time was short before she would have to leave too. She left the room to pray for one more opportunity to share Jesus with her grandma. She took a deep breath. Armed with her Bible and a new courage, she walked into Grandma's room. Once again, she asked, "Grandma, wouldn't you like to receive Jesus and spend eternity in heaven with him?"

Between her writhing and cries of agony, Grandma Wilma screamed, "Take your Jesus and your Bible and get out of here!"

Anna Joy departed, heartbroken. She cried out to the Lord, "Why did you send me to her? She completely rejected you!"

She heard a whisper in her spirit, "How do you know what happened after you left?"

She continued to pray, remembering the wages of the workers who accepted the Lord's offer at the last hour and the thief who trusted in God while hanging on the cross.

46.

A New Direction

The LORD says, "I will guide you along the best pathway
for your life. I will advise you and watch over you."

Psalm 32:8 (NLT)

"I think the Lord is telling me to quit my job." Anna Joy swirled another forkful of spaghetti before looking up at Debra, seated across the table from her.

Debra stopped her fork in midair. "That's a huge decision."

"By the end of the day, my legs are swollen like sausages, and the calf cramps are keeping me awake at night." She drew in a deep breath. "Since the management at the bank changed, my breaks are erratic. Sometimes no one comes for my breaks, so I'm not able to get to the bathroom on time." She looked down at her plate. "It's worse when I don't get a lunch break." She didn't want to tell Debra that, even though she wasn't quite forty, she had become increasingly short of breath with walking.

"I know they've made work hard for you. How do you plan to support yourself?"

"I think the Lord wants me to live by faith. He says he wants the body of Christ to take care of me." She sniggered. "God, I can trust. I'm not sure about people."

"That's a big step. You could probably get disability."

"I know. He also said I'm not supposed to take any government money. I've lived by faith before. But it hasn't always been easy."

"What will you do?"

"I think the Lord wants me to spend more time in prayer and counseling. I already counsel a lot of people you don't know about, especially by phone."

.୰ঌৡৡ঳.

Anna Joy knew the time had come to give her supervisor a six-month notice as the Lord had instructed. She walked into his office and handed him her resignation.

"We're sorry to lose you, Anna Joy. You've done a wonderful job. I could always count on you." He smiled. "I will miss your pleasant voice when you page us."

"I'll make sure my replacement will have everything they need. I'll create a manual for you with all the phone numbers, extensions, and the information they need to do my job, so the next person will have an easier transition."

After she gave her resignation, she turned her attention to creating the manual. For the next six months, she spent her spare time painstakingly writing phone numbers and instructions. For several years already, she could only write for short periods of time since her fingers would develop painful cramps.

On her last day of work, she could finally enjoy the remnants of her going-away party during her late lunch break. She had hoped the management would give her a couple of weeks to train her replacement. But as far as she knew, they had not hired anyone to take her place at the switchboard.

Friends had promised financial support, but most of the people she knew were college students or families living on a shoestring budget. A few refused to offer any support since she refused to take government money. God would have to supply her needs.

.ₒᴥₒ.

She didn't realize how much effort her job cost her until she resigned. She was tired. But she enjoyed counseling people on the phone and those who came to her apartment when her mom was at work. She loved to talk about Jesus, study the Bible, and pray for people to live in the freedom Christ offered. She also enjoyed the time she had for intercessory prayer, which she felt was her primary ministry.

.ₒᴥₒ.

One day, Anna Joy greeted her mom when she returned home from work. "How was your day?"

After her mom hung up her coat, she pulled a cigarette out of her purse and wedged it between her lips. "Well, I got the payroll done." She foraged in her purse, drew out a lighter, and lit the cigarette. "I'm glad it's Friday." She blew out a puff of smoke. "You know, I've been working since I was eighteen, and I think I'm going to retire next year."

"That's great, Mom. You deserve a break." Anna Joy quickly did the math. How could she continue to counsel if her mom was home all day? Her mom had no outside activities or interests besides television soap operas. Anna Joy enjoyed having the apartment to herself during the day and the freedom to help people from her home. Besides, with her mother home all day, the apartment would become so smoke-filled from her mother's chain smoking that Anna Joy would have difficulty breathing.

Lord, I need your help.

47.

The Forty-Day Retreat

Rise up, my love, my fair one, And come away!

Song of Solomon 2:13 (NKJV)

Anna Joy and her pastor slid into the booth at her favorite restaurant. Ever since she had accepted a leadership position in the prayer group, she sensed the Lord leading her to meet monthly with a spiritual director.

Her pastor picked up his roll. "I like to eat the roll first while it's still warm." He took a bite. "Have you considered going on a forty-day retreat?"

"I've never thought about it. I'm not sure where I'd go." She cut into her ribeye, which she preferred over the roll.

"Well, you can go anywhere as long as you leave town, so you're not distracted. It's a life-changing experience. I highly recommend it."

"How does one do a forty-day retreat?"

"For the first three days, you do absolutely nothing. You don't open your Bible or any other books the Lord leads you to bring. You don't even pray, which is the hardest part. You wait for God to show up." He plucked a forkful of steak and slipped it into his mouth. "This steak is good. By the way, you also fast for the forty days. I usually do a juice fast."

"That's a long time to fast." Fasting wasn't new to Anna Joy. Sister Gladys had encouraged frequent bouts of fasting during their times of ministry together.

Anna Joy sensed the Lord inviting her to enter into a forty-day retreat with him. She knew one didn't usually have contact with other people on these retreats, but she couldn't physically manage being alone for that length of time without extra support. Maybe Allen would help her. He had relocated to California to continue his education. After Anna Joy told him about her plans, he offered to help her find a place to stay and assist her with whatever she needed during her retreat.

.ᴄ᠑ᵉᴐ.

Even though Anna Joy was tired from travel, her face lit up when she spotted Allen at the airport. She had looked forward to seeing him again.

Allen flashed her a smile and strode toward her. "I'm so glad you're here. I found you a nice motel not too far from me for your retreat." He grabbed her luggage with one hand and wheeled her out to the car with the other. Before settling her into the motel, he took her out for a light dinner.

Anna Joy scanned the extended-stay motel room, her home for the next forty days. Besides a bed, the accessible room included a worn couch, a desk, and a chair. The kitchenette would accommodate her needs for a juice fast.

Allen helped her unpack. He placed the juice, which he had purchased prior to her arrival, in the refrigerator. "I'll stop back tomorrow to check on you." He set a Coke and glass of water on the bedside table. "Are you set for the night?"

Anna Joy took a deep breath and then nodded. She wasn't sure she was set, but she couldn't think of anything else she needed. The door clicked shut. *Well, Lord, here I am.*

The next morning, she brewed a cup of coffee. Not because she liked coffee, but she hoped the warm liquid would prevent the chills she usually experienced when fasting. She set her coffee on the bedside table and tossed her pillows onto the floor next to the bed. She slid to the floor and rested her back against the pillows. What was she supposed to do now? Her pastor told her to just sit and wait on God. But how does one just wait?

She scanned the room, hoping there was something she could look at besides the beige walls and faded pictures. Her eyes rested on one of the books she brought. No, reading a book was not on her pastor's list of doing nothing. She dozed and waited some more. She was more tired than she thought. Toward evening, she heard a knock and the click of a key in the door.

Allen walked in. "How are you? Do you want me to heat up the vegetable juice for you?"

"I'm okay. I'm not sure what I was supposed to do today, but I'm here." She flashed him a wan smile. Allen heated the juice on the stove and then handed her the warm mug, a routine they fell into for the next forty days.

By the fourth day of the retreat, Anna Joy sensed the presence of the Lord. He directed her to various Bible passages and gave her new revelations and insights into his Word. She loved God-led Bible studies where he would direct her from one passage to another.

She sensed the joy of God's tangible presence. Sometimes she worshipped, and other times she sat in his silence, awed by his majesty. His love and peace enveloped her.

The benefits of fasting were not just spiritual. As the fasting retreat progressed, her clothes felt looser. The pain and cramping in her legs diminished as the swelling in her body decreased.

One day, the Lord gave her a picture of an antique treasure chest. As the moving picture unfolded, she watched herself carefully lift the rounded lid of the chest. Jewels spilled from the chest: rubies, emeralds, amethysts, and sapphires in a myriad of shapes, sizes, and colors. Their dazzling brilliance nearly blinded her. As her eyes adjusted to the radiance, she noticed letters engraved on each gemstone. She recognized names of friends, family members, and acquaintances inscribed on them.

As she picked through the array of precious stones, she noticed that some of the jewels were etched with names she didn't recognize. "Who are these people, Lord?"

The Lord whispered, "These precious jewels represent those lives you have invested in, the people you have loved, and those you have interceded for. Some you do not yet know. Others you won't meet until you join me in glory."

As the vision faded, Anna Joy rested against her pillows, awed that God shared with her that which is most precious to him: the people he created for his glory. Yes, these were the priceless treasures she would one day carry to the throne of her King. The true measure of her wealth—the lives she had touched.

Toward the end of her retreat, memories bombarded her mind in rapid succession. God spoke to her about her life and the lives of her spiritual children.

It seemed as if the Lord had parted a veil and revealed a glimpse into her future. A future filled with the joy of current and future relationships. But the Lord also warned her that she would experience betrayal and loss. And she would suffer much.

The truth of the Word, the revelation of Jesus, and the joy she experienced in his presence during those forty days sustained her for the rest of her life.

48.

The Move

I will lead a life of integrity in my own home.

Psalm 101:2 (NLT)

Debra walked into Anna Joy's apartment, dropped her coat, and flopped onto the couch. "I need to find another place to live."

"I'll pray that you find the right place. I can go with you to look at places. I want to be sure it's a nice place for you," Anna Joy said.

Anna Joy trudged into one apartment after another with Debra. Some were dives, and a few worth a second look. But there was one place, a new complex, they both liked. The manager seemed nice, and the complex staffed an on-site office. They would pray about Debra taking that apartment.

As Anna Joy looked for an apartment with Debra, an idea toyed in her mind. Maybe she and Debra could live together. They were best friends.

Since her mother had retired, Anna Joy found it difficult to continue her biblical counseling ministry from her home. If she lived with Debra, that would not be an issue. She knew Debra supported her ministry. But what would her mother say? She needed her mom to agree. Even though Mom didn't know Jesus like she did, Anna Joy respected the authority God had placed over her as a mother.

Anna Joy prayed and took a deep breath before approaching her mother. "Mom, I was wondering what you'd say to my moving into an apartment with Debra."

"Well, it might be nice for you to live with someone closer to your age. Have you found a place you like?"

"Yes, we found a nice two-bedroom, two-bathroom apartment on the first floor. It's brand new." Besides, this apartment had a real bathtub. All the other apartments had fiberglass tubs. Anna Joy didn't like fiberglass. She was afraid of falling and breaking the tub.

"Do you think you can afford it?"

Anna Joy nodded. If her mother agreed, she knew God would provide.

"Well, I guess that would be okay."

Anna Joy called Debra. "I can't believe she said yes! This must be God! Let's go back and sign the lease before she changes her mind."

Debra and Anna Joy walked into the office of the apartment complex. "We'd like to rent the apartment we looked at."

"I'm sorry, but we already rented that apartment, but we have another first-floor apartment you might like."

Anna Joy sighed, her face crestfallen. "I guess we can look at it." First floor was important for her in case the elevator broke or there was a fire. She was afraid of fire.

The manager grabbed the keys and her coat and led them out the door. "This apartment is very similar to the other one, it's a corner unit that faces south, so it's very bright and cheery."

They walked in and knew this was the apartment God had chosen for them. The Lord knew that this apartment met her needs better than the original one. The entrance to this building had no steps.

Anna Joy and Debra signed the lease.

.୦ଚ୍ଚ.

"Mom! Debra and I found an apartment, and we signed the lease! We'll be moving in next month."

"I wish you weren't moving." Anna Joy's mother lit her cigarette and took a puff. "I don't know why I said yes." She pursed her lips and looked over toward her daughter.

"I know. But I've already signed the lease." It was too late to change her mind. God had ordained this move. Anna Joy rejoiced that she and Debra were moving in together.

·⌒∾⌒·

"Debra, can you go to the store and buy some candy for me?" Anna Joy asked.

"What kind of candy?"

"All different kinds of miniatures. I want a candy jar so I can offer the kids candy when they come." Anna Joy loved children and enjoyed their visits. "They can each take three pieces."

Usually the children accepted her three-limit rule. But one day her three-year-old goddaughter had reached her fingers into the jar and selected her three pieces just as her siblings had done. A short time later she bounded back into Anna Joy's room, requesting more candy. Anna Joy shook her head. "No, you've had your three pieces."

The child's wail drew her older brother into the room. "What's wrong?"

"She's already had her three pieces of candy and wants more."

"You might as well stop crying. Three's the limit and she won't change her mind." He took her hand and led his sniffling sister out of the room.

"It's important to keep your word, even with something so trivial as three pieces of candy from the candy jar," Anna Joy said.

·⌒∾⌒·

Anna Joy wrote to a friend:

> Debra and I finally found an apartment for both of us:
> two bedrooms, two baths. The kidney-bladder demands
> a bathroom connected to my bedroom, plus more. It's
> worse, and finding accessible housing is very difficult.
> This is beautiful.
>
> Now all I have to do is to trust the Lord to supply many
> needed things. The location allows me to walk to
> shopping, restaurants, the bank, and post office, etc. It
> also gives me several other choices to get outside: a lawn
> gazebo, pool, patio, and terrace. I needed to move because
> I can no longer counsel at home with mom home all day.
> Besides, God seemed to speak, generally of a move, and
> I counseled with many who know me in various places
> and capacities, based on Proverbs 15:22 (NKJV): "Without
> counsel, plans go awry, But in the multitude of counselors
> they are established." Their separate counsel agreed. It's
> scary for me. The lease is for a year.
>
> God is teaching me, and others through me, the
> relationship between holiness and love. I have to say
> learning about the correlation made me aware of how
> often I don't act or think lovingly, or in a holy, i.e. like
> Jesus's, manner. The counseling and teaching keep me
> busy. There are many needs in my life. I would appreciate
> your prayers so Jesus may be glorified in me.

49.

Liberty and *Les Misérables*

Ask and you will receive, and your joy will be complete.

John 16:24 (NIV)

Years before, as a college student, Anna Joy had laid a thick novel in her lap and rubbed her eyes. She'd devoured the English version of *Les Misérables* in high school, and now she had tackled the book in French for her college French class. "Lord, would you arrange for me to see a musical version of *Les Misérables* on Broadway?" she'd prayed.

However, in the 1960s, no musical score had yet been composed for *Les Misérables*.

.⧬.

Many years later, her prayer group friends, Aaron and Miriam, invited Anna Joy to visit them out East. While they toured the historic district of Philadelphia, a white horse-drawn carriage clip-clopped past them.

"Can we go for a carriage ride?" Anna Joy's gaze followed the regal horse and coachman.

The gold-gilded white carriage pulled to a stop in front of them. Aaron helped Anna Joy and Miriam up the steps and seated them in the red velvet seat. They rode through the narrow cobblestone streets lined with red brick sidewalks. Anna Joy felt like royalty.

After the ride, Aaron pushed her in her wheelchair to the Liberty Bell. She ran her finger over the crack in the bronze bell and read the inscription, "Proclaim LIBERTY Throughout All the Land Unto All the Inhabitants Thereof."

Next they entered Independence Hall, where their forefathers had signed the Declaration of Independence. Anna Joy marveled at the historic significance of the hall as she scanned the room. Two antique captain's chairs, marred by scratches, were positioned at each desk shrouded with a green cloth. She stared at the copies of the parchment documents written by the founding fathers. Their bold signatures could have cost them their lives.

The next day, the trio headed to New York City via a dimly lit tunnel beneath the Hudson River. Anna Joy had never traveled under a river. *What if the walls cave?*

Finally, they arrived in New York City with its double-parking, beeping horns, and taxis weaving in and out of traffic. Jarred again and again by the slamming of brakes, Anna Joy prayed and thanked God she wasn't driving.

At the pier, she marveled at the Statue of Liberty protruding from the water, a bastion of freedom visible for miles.

Aaron pushed her up the ramp into the waiting ferry, a double treat since she loved boat rides and had never been to Lady Liberty. She drew her cape tighter as the cold breeze nipped at her neck. The ferry seemed to glide over the waves.

At the base of the statue, a museum featuring true-to-size bronze images of Lady Liberty's face, feet, and torch greeted the visitors. Anna Joy reached out and stroked the replicas of Liberty's smooth face and toes. She stared up at the circular staircase leading to the torch, approximately twenty stories high. Hardly room for one to ascend, let alone for another person to pass at the same time. She could climb stairs, but not this staircase.

As evening approached, they drove through New York's theater district. Many of the theaters were nondescript brick buildings plastered with huge marquees announcing the current Broadway productions. She couldn't fathom how these plain buildings could house elegant theaters with velvet curtains concealing a stage.

Anna Joy gasped when she spotted the marquee announcing *Les Misérables*, featuring the image of the young Cosette. God had answered her prayers—*Les Misérables*, the musical. But she still hadn't seen it.

She recalled the first time she heard about *Les Misérables* on Broadway. In 1980, the French musical version of *Les Misérables* first appeared on stage in Paris. The English version first played in London in 1985 and on Broadway in 1987. Even now, several years later, *Les Misérables* was the most popular show on Broadway.

Anna Joy turned toward Aaron, her voice filled with hope. "Can we go see *Les Misérables*? It's my favorite book."

"I can't go this week, but I'll try to get tickets for next week."

Anna Joy knew that patrons had been purchasing tickets months in advance. She prayed. *Please, Lord, let him be able to get tickets.*

A few days later, Aaron came home from work. "How was your day?"

Miriam looked up as she prepped supper with Anna Joy's help. "We stopped by the crystal shop and then picked up Anna Joy's green leather purse she ordered from the Bag Lady. How was yours?"

Aaron foraged in the cabinets. "Good. My PhD student seems to be catching on." He found a cookie and took a bite. "By the way, I got tickets for *Les Misérables*."

Anna Joy cried out, nearly dropping the paring knife she held in her hand. "We're really going to *Les Misérables*?"

The next week, they embarked on another trip to New York City. Aaron dropped Miriam and Anna Joy off at the door to the theater and parked the car.

As Miriam pushed her wheelchair into the theater, Anna Joy gawked at the crystal chandeliers hung from the vaulted ceiling. Rows of box seats lined the perimeter of the theater.

Miriam followed the usher down the aisle. They passed row after row of plush red theater seats.

A few rows back from the stage, the usher stopped. "Here are your seats."

Miriam maneuvered the wheelchair into the open space on the aisle. She slipped past Anna Joy and took her seat. Aaron was seated a few rows back.

Anna Joy opened her program, careful not to rumple the pages. She studied the faces of the actors and their profiles. People chatted excitedly as they filed into the theater.

As the orchestra played the first strains of the musical score, Anna Joy closed her eyes, transported to a different time and a different place.

She recoiled at the injustice of the prison sentence inflicted upon Jean Valjean for stealing a loaf of bread to feed his sister's starving family. The plights of Fantine and her young daughter, Cosette, grieved her heart. As Eponine sang "On My Own," tears trickled down Anna Joy's cheeks. Eponine's heartbreak resonated with Anna Joy's own losses.

But the bishop was her favorite character. The bishop represented redemption and forgiveness. After the bishop housed and fed Jean Valjean, the constable caught him stealing the bishop's silver. However, the bishop did the unthinkable. He gave Jean Valjean the stolen items plus his silver candlesticks. This act of mercy and love transformed Jean Valjean.

After the finale, the cast backed away amid uproarious applause. The curtain dropped, and Anna Joy sank into her seat. She blinked as the house lights flickered on, and she was catapulted back into her present-day reality.

Miriam pushed Anna Joy out of the auditorium while Aaron

retrieved the car. The marquee lights canceled the darkness of night as they waited on the sidewalk.

A middle-aged man exited the theater and stopped near Anna Joy and Miriam. "How did you like the performance?"

"It was wonderful!" Anna Joy hugged her souvenir program. "*Les Misérables* is my favorite book."

The man smiled. "I'm so glad. I'm the bishop."

Anna Joy gasped. "The bishop is my favorite character! Without the bishop, there would be no story."

Aaron pulled up to the curb.

As Anna Joy climbed into the car, she cried out and pointed to the man's retreating form. "We met the bishop!" In the persona of the bishop, she felt as though she had encountered Father God.

50.

A Change of Heart

Honor your father and your mother, as the LORD your God has
commanded you, so that you may live long and that it may go
well with you in the land the LORD your God is giving you.

Deuteronomy 5:16 (NIV)

"Can I come over? Now?" Anna Joy's voice quavered. She swallowed, waiting for Benny's response.

"Of course! What's wrong?" A disconnect beep answered him.

With tears streaming down her cheeks, Anna Joy walked through the door of Benny's family home, crawled under the dining room table, and cowered in a corner.

"Anna Joy?" Benny crouched down and peered under the table. "What's going on?" He stretched his hand toward her. "Come on out. Talk to me."

She shook her head, huddled in a fetal position. "A relative called," she cried. "My dad's in town for the weekend." She hadn't heard from him since her grandma passed away. "Dad's been drinking and has a gun. He says he wants to kill me! I've known for a long time he's had a gun for protection, but I never thought he would turn it on me!" She curled up tighter in response to Benny's repeated attempts to coax her out.

"Why does he want to kill you?"

"I know he resents the cerebral palsy, but I didn't think he hated me enough to kill me!" She knew he blamed her for the disability. According to him, Anna Joy stole his wife's attention and affection from him, eventually leading to their divorce. Current financial struggles and yet another divorce had only fueled his rage, especially when he was drinking, and reminded him he had lost the love of his life—Anna Joy's mom.

Benny joined her under the table and wrapped his arms around her shoulders. "You can come out and stay here as long as you need to. You're safe here."

"I'm afraid to go home!" She whimpered and grabbed tissues from the box Benny's wife slid under the table. "I'm such a coward!" Anna Joy banged her fist on the carpet. "A worthless, worthless coward!" Sobs racked her frame. Tears from years of pain and rejection soaked his shirt.

The day wore on into night. She refused to budge except to lift her head as her friends slipped a pillow beneath her tear-stained cheek and tucked blankets around her. Eventually she fell asleep underneath the old oak table that represented many happy gatherings with family and friends.

She called her mom the next day. "Hi, Mom. I heard Dad was in town. Did you get to see him?" Anna Joy tried to sound cheerful.

"I went to dinner with him and had a nice visit. But he was planning to leave today."

Anna Joy drew in a deep breath and sighed. She could head back to her apartment. She didn't tell her mom about the gun or hiding at Benny's.

While she didn't meet with her father then, she also refused to cut off all contact with him. Year after year, she sent him notes and cards, even though he never responded.

·⁓∘⁓·

Anna Joy set aside the notecard she'd been writing. Her fingers needed a break. She picked up a nearby stack of cards and shuffled through them. She turned to Debra who had appeared in the doorway. "Can you get me a Father's Day card?"

"Who do you want to send a Father's Day card to?"

"I want to send one to my dad." Anna Joy refused to meet Debra's gaze.

"How can you send your dad a Father's Day card after all he's done to you?" With her hands on her hips, Debra glared at Anna Joy. "He threatened to kill you! Besides, most of the cards say something like, 'You are a wonderful, loving father.' Well, that's a bald-faced lie!"

Anna Joy paused and picked up the pen she'd been using to scrawl her latest note. "That was a while ago, and he hasn't threatened me since then. Besides, I've forgiven him. I tell him the truth—I love him. I'm not sure anyone ever really loved him. Maybe if I continue to reach out to him, he will someday realize that God loves him too. I send him birthday cards—when I can track his address. It changes a lot."

·⁓∘⁓·

One day, Anna Joy lay on the floor, wedged between her bed and cedar chest. She plumped the multiple pillows that propped her up and reached for her book. The phone jingled. "Hello?"

"Hi, Pumpkin. Happy birthday!"

"Dad! How are you?" She hadn't heard anything from him for years. Not a letter, not a phone call. How did he get her number?

They talked for several minutes. "Well, I'd better go now."

"I love you, Dad!" She managed to say before he hung up.

Anna Joy clapped her hands. "Thank you, Jesus! My birthday's not until tomorrow, but he remembered!" All those years of sending cards, keeping in touch with him, telling him she loved him, had finally paid off. Her love and forgiveness had paved the road to reconciliation. A reconciliation she hoped would eventually include God.

51.

An Alaskan Adventure

*Let heaven and earth praise Him, The seas
and everything that moves in them.*

Psalm 69:34 (NKJV)

One day, a friend waved a brochure as she entered Anna Joy's and Debra's living room. "How would you like to go on a cruise to Alaska with one of our favorite Bible teachers? Between seeing the sights, we'll have Bible teachings and Christian concerts."

Anna Joy accepted the brochure and flipped it open. "Wow, this sounds like fun."

Debra scanned the brochure's seven-day itinerary through Alaska's Inside Passage, noting several ports of call and whale watching in Glacier Bay. "Why don't we go? The full payment isn't due for a while. We'll have enough time to save our money for the trip."

Anna Joy agreed. *Lord, if this trip is from you, you'll have to provide the money for me to go.*

.⸎⸎⸎.

After several connecting flights, the three friends arrived at the cruise terminal with their multiple oversized suitcases in tow. Once

223

again, Anna Joy riffled through her purse and fingered her boarding documents. She looked around the great room, lined with multiple signs overlooking various check-in counters. So many people. So many lines. *Where are we supposed to go?*

They spotted their counter, checked in, and followed the signs to board their ship. Debra pushed Anna Joy's chair up the ship's gangway. Once on board, a flash from the camera held by the ship's photographer nearly blinded Anna Joy's travel-weary eyes.

A crew member guided them to their assigned quarters. He opened the door, revealing a small cabin with three beds and a porthole window. "We'll bring your luggage a little later."

"Let's go up on deck and watch the ship pull away," Debra said. She grasped the wheelchair, and the trio searched for signs leading to the open deck. They joined the other passengers laughing and chatting on deck as they jostled for positions at the rail, awaiting departure. Their excitement surged as the ship's horn bellowed, and the vessel slowly pulled away from the dock. Anchors aweigh!

Between scheduled teachings during their first day at sea, they strolled the deck and inhaled the fresh, crisp air. Only the hum of the ship's engine interrupted this pristine environment. Anna Joy was amazed at how the ship glided with ease through shimmering waters surrounded by miles of mountains seemingly untouched by man's hands.

That evening they joined the rest of their group in the Admiral's Lounge for the Captain's Party, to be followed by the first of two formal dinners. Anna Joy wheeled herself over to the vases overflowing with floral arrangements. "Have you ever seen such beautiful flowers? They're everywhere we turn. And so many varieties: mums, carnations, lilies, and roses. Even bird of paradise!" She stuck her nose into the bouquet of flowers and sniffed. "They smell heavenly." When her dinner arrived, she almost didn't want to disturb its lovely presentation, but she succumbed. Her steak nearly melted in her mouth.

Seven o'clock arrived way too early the next day. But their scheduled seaplane excursion awaited them at their first port of call—Ketchikan. Anna Joy donned her new mint-green running suit, which she had purchased specifically for the trip. Amid a light drizzle, they boarded the smaller tender boat and headed for shore.

Once there, Anna Joy stared at the seaplane as it pitched to and fro over the choppy waves. How was she going to board? With the help of the pilot, she clung to the metal rungs of the ladder and threw her body onto the grimy floor of the bobbing plane. She pulled herself up and pivoted into the seat. Once settled, Anna Joy glanced down at the front of her running suit and grimaced. Blackened grease stained the front of her clothes from top to bottom. Her new outfit was ruined.

Her heart raced in tandem with the motor as the plane sailed across the sea and lifted off into the Misty Fjords, a coastal rainforest formed by glacial and volcanic activity. As they entered the fjords, a double rainbow welcomed them. She put her nose to the windowpane and drank in the surrounding beauty. White mist clung to the snow-capped peaks like a fine smoke film. Waterfalls tumbled down cliffs into blue glacial lakes surrounded by rich foliage.

When she returned to the ship, people she had never met greeted her and congratulated Anna Joy on her courage and adventuresome spirit. "We couldn't believe you got on that plane!" someone said.

"How did you know about that?"

"Oh, word about you reached the ship long before you returned. You're famous!"

Anna Joy glanced down at her soiled clothes and blushed.

A new port and a new adventure awaited them the next day. Anna Joy and Debra boarded a bus for a tour of Juneau. They stopped at the Mendenhall Glacier, which dates back to the Ice Age. The blue-tinged ice zigzagged through the mountains as far as her eyes could see. Anna Joy watched the occasional chunks of ice bob in the Mendenhall River, which flowed past the glacier. They scanned the river, hoping to catch a glimpse of their friend who had gone river rafting.

Before the bus returned to town, it wound around the highway until the road abruptly ended at the base of a mountain.

After exiting the bus, they boarded a catamaran for a four-hour cruise up the Lynn Canal to Skagway, a gold rush town. For centuries, trappers, traders, and fortune seekers traversed this glacial fjord. Anna Joy settled back in her seat and enjoyed the serenity of her surroundings. Multiple waterfalls cascaded down lush green mountainsides and splashed into the canal. "Look!" She laughed and pointed to the porpoises that skimmed over their wake.

For a change of scenery, she walked around the vessel and eventually gravitated toward the jewelry displayed in the small onboard gift shop. Anna Joy loved jewelry, especially emeralds. Her rings, brooches, and necklaces were among the few things she couldn't destroy if she fell. Her eyes were drawn to the rack of crystal necklaces. "Look at the rainbows!" The sunlight played on the facets of crystal and created rainbows that danced in its rays. From the first time she hung a faceted piece of crystal in her window, she was captivated by the spectrum of colors caused by the dispersion of light. She selected a crystal necklace in greens and blues, which she dubbed her Alaskan crystal.

After a brief tour and dinner in Skagway, they boarded a six-passenger aircraft and flew over the ice caps of Juneau, which resembled fields of crackled glass. Anna Joy marveled at the streams of water flowing down ragged cliffs and spilling into the rivers below. Between snow-capped mountain peaks, the setting sun glimmered in shades of gold.

They returned as darkness encroached upon downtown Juneau. "I want to stop at one more place before we go back to the ship. I've always wanted a fur coat." Anna Joy pointed to a shop displaying an array of fur coats and hats in their window. A friend had given her extra money and told her to buy something special for herself. "That store looks open."

Once inside, she scanned the racks of fur coats: fox, beaver, mink, and muskrat. How would she ever choose just one? She tried on several coats and finally selected a muskrat fur as well as a beaver hat. The shopkeeper agreed to ship them to Anna Joy's home.

The next day, they entered Glacier Bay. Anna Joy and her friends joined the other passengers on deck as they glided past Margerie Glacier. The director told them that centuries of snow-packed ice extended one hundred feet below the waterline, soared two hundred fifty feet high, and spanned twenty-one miles. Every so often, a blue-tinged glacial chunk rumbled as it broke off and crashed into the water. Harbor seals sunned themselves on these remnants of calved icebergs scattered throughout the bay.

With binoculars poised on the brims of their noses, the tourists scanned the horizon, searching for humpback whales. In the distance, someone spotted several plumes of water spouting from their blowholes. Occasionally the whales breached. Anna Joy clapped and squealed as the whales leaped, hauling their enormous bodies out of the water. Would they come close enough to splash her as their barnacled backsides smacked the water's surface?

Before their trip ended, the group visited one more port of call: Sitka, an island community nestled between the mountains and the sea. As Anna Joy looked around the city, she noted that this city was different. It had a distinctly Russian flair intermingled with the culture of the native Eskimos. Downtown Sitka featured a Russian Orthodox church, complete with an onion dome typically included in Russian architectural designs.

Anna Joy pointed to a museum-type building. "Let's go in there. There is a program starting soon." They entered the building and were directed to a theater featuring Russian costumes and dancers. After the program, they stopped at the gift shop. Russian nesting dolls lined one of the shelves alongside fishing and Native American memorabilia.

The last evening on board ship, the passengers enjoyed a concert with well-known Christian artists, followed by last-minute instructions from the crew. "Leave your suitcases outside the door tonight. We will collect them and return them to you after you disembark. Be sure to set aside anything you need for tomorrow. You don't want to be like the man who had to be escorted off the ship wrapped in a blanket." The audience chuckled.

No blanket wraps for this trio as the anchor dropped for the final time.

52.

A Visit to the Reservations

I will thank you, Lord, among all the people. I will
sing your praises among the nations.

Psalm 57:9 (NLT)

"Guess what, Debra?" Anna Joy cradled the phone. "That was my cousin, Sister Dorothy. She invited us to visit her on the reservation where she teaches."

Several weeks later, as rain pelted their vehicle, Debra and Anna Joy drove along a dark, forested highway through the Menominee reservation. Anna Joy breathed a sigh of relief when they finally arrived at Sister Dorothy's convent.

"You made it!" Sister Dorothy grinned and hugged Anna Joy. "Let me show you to your rooms. There used to be more nuns living here, but now those vacant rooms are our guest rooms."

That evening, Anna Joy reminisced with Sister Dorothy. "You were fifteen and I was seven when you entered the convent. I wanted to be a nun just like you and wear the long black habit and veil. I remember the day we went to the cathedral and watched you take your vows. I was afraid I couldn't find you amid all the other nuns dressed in their white bridal gowns. After you took your vows, I was so sad that the convent wouldn't let us see you anymore. I'm glad that's changed now."

Sister Dorothy laughed. "I'm glad too. We didn't even get to see our parents very often back then."

The next day, Sister Dorothy gave them a tour of their small elementary school, sparsely supplied but clean. A few of the Menominee children climbed on the rusty playground equipment. They barely glanced at the newcomers before resuming their play.

"It's not safe to walk anywhere on the reservation without one of us with you," Sister Dorothy cautioned as they toured the reservation. "The people are familiar with us but suspicious of strangers."

Anna Joy's wheelchair bounced over the hard, dry ground. How could anything grow here? She stared at the huts strewn across the reservation. A woman, perched on a stool outside her hut, looked up briefly before stirring her pot on the outdoor cookstove. Another woman with a faded shawl draped over her shoulders sat huddled outside her hovel weaving reeds into a basket. How did these families stay warm during the bitter cold winters?

That evening, one of the nuns picked up a tiny bead from a tray and wove it into the beaded pattern she was working into a key ring. "Did you know the Native Americans leave a little imperfection in whatever item they make? This is their way of acknowledging that only God is perfect."

.ୖୡୖ.

A few years later, Sister Dorothy's religious order transferred her to a school on a reservation in Arizona. Once again, she invited Anna Joy and Debra to come for a visit.

Anna Joy greeted her cousin at the airport. "Sister, you're all dressed in white."

"The motherhouse allows us to trade in our black skirts and veils for white because of the Arizona climate. Unfortunately, the white is much harder to keep clean in all this dust."

As they drove to the reservation, Anna Joy scanned the sandy landscape dotted with various species of cacti: saguaro, organ pipe, cholla, and prickly pear. Downy fluffs of cotton clung to shrubs in a cotton field. When they entered the reservation, Sister Dorothy pointed out a small cluster of ramshackle houses. "Many of the homes here are built out of ironwood, mesquite, and the woody part of the saguaro cacti. The small wooden pens are for the chickens or small livestock."

The reservation seemed to extend for miles, desolate and barren except for the prickly cacti. Anna Joy heard mooing nearby. Men were loading a herd of baby bulls into a long truck. Where did the cattle come from? She couldn't see any grazeable grass.

As she stepped out of the car, the dry, dusty heat clogged her sinuses. She spotted a large orange-and-black snake slithering on the other side of the rusty fence that surrounded the convent property. She paused.

"Don't worry. He won't hurt you. That's just a milk snake. They eat the mice and rats." Sister Dorothy escorted them to their rooms in the modest adobe convent. "Be sure to shake out your shoes before putting them on. Scorpions love to hide in dark places."

Anna Joy spotted what appeared to be a baby scorpion scurry across the floor. Mice, rats, and scorpions. Yuck. She'd also have to remain alert for tarantulas and black widow spiders. She hadn't changed her opinion about spiders.

While Anna Joy and Debra settled in, Sister Dorothy collected the laundry from the clothesline. "It's so arid, our sheets dry in about an hour. Be sure to drink a lot of water. You can get dehydrated quickly here and not realize it." She wiped her reddened face.

The next day, they toured the reservation with Sister Dorothy. Children clambered around a swing set anchored into the sandy playground at the Native American school. A few boys shot hoops on the concrete basketball court.

"This is our mission church." Sister Dorothy opened the heavy wooden doors of the adobe structure. A bronze bell hung from a small bell tower encased in brick. Rows of wooden pews lined either side of the center aisle, facing the altar. "During Mass on Sunday, you'll find the parishioners come in at various times. They don't have the same sense of Western time like we do." She shrugged. "But at least they come. Many still practice ancestor worship. They take full advantage of their favorite holy day, All Souls' Day. They prepare special food to take to the gravesides of their ancestors."

They resumed their tour of the grounds. Sister Dorothy pointed to a dilapidated adobe building. "That's the old mission church. We can go inside, but be careful. Some of the floorboards are rotting. It's supposed to be torn down later this year."

They stepped into the church and crept across the creaking floorboards. Anna Joy squinted in the sunlight peeking through the rotting rafters. A vase of fresh flowers graced the side of the simple wooden altar. Above the altar, a fresco of the Last Supper covered the wall. Jesus, with a golden halo and clad in white, held a small loaf of bread. The twelve apostles, wearing brightly colored garments in shades of greens, blues, reds, and yellows, surrounded a round table covered with an embroidered white tablecloth. Their faces, which featured Native American characteristics, gazed heavenward, except the face of Judas. He grasped a moneybag, his back turned toward Jesus. How sad that this beautiful fresco would be destroyed when they tore down the church.

Anna Joy scanned the expanse of the barren landscape. "It's so depressing here. Do people ever get off the reservation?"

"A few. Unemployment is high here, so some work off the reservation and send money home. But eventually they return to their families and their traditions. The culture outside of the tribe is so different that many find it hard to fit in. Extended family and traditions are important in the Native American culture. Besides, this is their home."

53.

A Safari—Texas Style

*I know every bird on the mountains, and all
the animals of the field are mine.*

Psalm 50:11 (NLT)

"How would you like to go on a safari?" Gert grinned as she set the table for a special dinner in honor of Anna Joy's visit. Debra had traveled with Anna Joy to visit her friends in Texas.

"A safari?" Anna Joy furrowed her brow. "Wouldn't we have to go to Africa?"

"You're not going to believe this, but there's actually a drive-through safari about an hour away."

The next day, a ranger greeted the trio as they arrived at the safari park entrance. "Welcome to the park. We have a few rules we need you to follow." He pointed to a sign. "Stay on the main road and drive slowly. And stay in your vehicle." He handed each of them a cardboard bucket of animal food. "Just stick the bucket out the window and the wildlife will come right to you. Only feed the animals with the food we provide. By the way, we are not responsible for any damage to your vehicle. Have a good day." He waved them through.

Gert set her bucket of food down and rolled up her window.

"The animals won't come if your window's closed," Debra said, rolling her window down.

"That's the whole point." Gert laughed. "I don't want animal slobber all over me."

A zebra lifted its head from a watering hole and moseyed across the sandy ground to their vehicle. Anna Joy held up her bucket. He stuck his nose into the container. As she pulled the bucket away, the zebra stepped closer and poked his whole head into the vehicle. She petted his snout. "I hope he doesn't bite!"

Gert eased the car away. Several impalas approached the vehicle, and one stuck his head through the window. Was he going to thrust his long horns in too? Thankfully the window was too small to accommodate those horns. He seemed to study Anna Joy with his large brown eyes. She held out her bucket, and he nibbled on the food pellets. Another impala nudged closer.

Bison, larger than their Pinto, grazed in the dry grasslands nearby along with some cattle. One of the bison attempted to stick its head through the window. But his head was too large to fit. Anna Joy tilted the bucket toward him, and he managed to scarf down the dregs. Good thing she had an extra bucket of food.

A longhorn cow poked her muzzle through the window. But her horns, which nearly spanned the length of the vehicle, prohibited further entry. She munched on whatever food she could reach and then sauntered away.

They passed by deer, geese, and giraffes as they followed the curves in the road. A small herd of camels grazed amid multiple feed buckets strewn along the roadside. "I can't believe people just tossed their buckets here. How rude!" Debra hung her bucket out the window. A camel approached her. He bared his teeth, yanked the bucket out of her hand, tilted his head back, and gulped its contents. After he drained the bucket, he flung his head and tossed the container aside. Her bucket now joined the other discarded containers. "Well, I guess that explains how all these buckets got here." Debra chuckled.

As they continued along the road, Debra said she felt a series of vibrations. "Look, a rhino!" A rhinoceros, larger than their small vehicle, trotted on the road just ahead of them. The ground trembled each time his hoof struck the pavement. "Part of his horn has been cut off. I wonder if they severed it so he can't gore anyone."

Before leaving the park, Anna Joy and Debra had also fed multiple species of antelope, buffalo, and cattle from their buckets. Gert laughed from the safety of her closed window. "I'll have to go through a car wash after this. Hopefully their horns didn't scrape my paint."

54.

The Healing Circuit

For to one is given the word of wisdom through the
Spirit, to another the word of knowledge through
the same Spirit, to another faith by the same Spirit,
to another gifts of healings by the same Spirit.

1 Corinthians 12:8-9 (NKJV)

Anna Joy squinted at the fuzzy picture that filled her television screen. The voice sounded familiar. Was he a preacher she had listened to while living in the Bible Belt? Oh, how she had missed these Bible teachers after she moved up north. Had she tuned in to a new Christian broadcast station? Eventually, the fuzzy picture cleared. "Lord, I know you did this just for me!"

After that, she tuned in to this station daily and became reacquainted with her beloved Bible teachers. She clung to their messages as they shared clips of miracles from their healing services. When they prayed for healing for their television audience at the end of their programs, she joined her prayers with theirs. Maybe God would heal her in her own bedroom.

One day she heard a healing ministry announce a crusade within driving distance. "Debra, let's go to this crusade. People are getting healed! Maybe God will heal me too!"

.ౢఎ෧ం.

Several months later, Debra and Anna Joy drove eight hours to attend the crusade. Anna Joy scanned the long line of wheelchairs while they waited for over two hours to enter the arena. So many sick and disabled people of all ages, strapped into their wheelchairs. Some transported crutches, oxygen, portable ventilators, and feeding tubes. All desperate to be healed.

The doors opened, and a crusade worker escorted them to the upper level of the arena and into one of the wheelchair seating areas. For the next two hours, Anna Joy watched the people crowd into the arena, their voices melding into an unrelieved cacophony. She squirmed. Fatigue nagged at her body.

When the orchestra opened the meeting, Anna Joy lifted her voice and joined the chorus of praises to God that echoed throughout the arena. During the final hymn, the healing evangelist walked out onto the platform. Anna Joy perched on the edge of her seat as he preached a message on God's healing power, followed by testimonies of various healings.

Then the atmosphere shifted. A hushed, reverent worship fell over the arena, welcoming the Holy Spirit. Soon the healing evangelist called out words of knowledge for various infirmities he sensed the Lord healing.

Anna Joy pulled herself out of the wheelchair and grasped the rail encircling the upper level. She closed her eyes and listened. *Is it my time, Lord?*

Soon, a worker rushed over to Anna Joy. "I was standing on the lower level, and when I looked up, I saw the presence of the Lord all over you! What is God doing for you?"

Anna Joy opened her eyes, startled by the woman's interruption. "I'm not sure. I just sense the Lord's presence."

The worker prayed for Anna Joy and then moved on.

After a time, the evangelist said, "Anyone who feels the Lord has healed them, come on down and form a line on either side of the platform."

People rose from all over the arena and flocked to the stage. Designated workers herded the crowds into the two lines. The woman sitting in the wheelchair next to Anna Joy unlocked her chair and slipped out.

Anna Joy sat back down in her chair. She listened as one person after another gave testimony of how God had healed them. Only the power of God could heal all the things wrong with her. She turned to Debra. "I'm glad for those who received healing, but I had hoped I would be one of those standing on the platform tonight."

Debra nodded. "Me too." She pointed to a woman standing on the platform. "Look! There's the woman who was sitting in the wheelchair right next to us!"

The woman raised her arms. "God has healed me from multiple sclerosis."

When the meeting ended, Anna Joy joined the others captive in their wheelchairs as they rolled through the arena and exited in silence. The shadows of night mingled with their disappointment.

This was the first of many cross-country trips by car and plane to Christian retreats, national conferences, and healing crusades in hopes of encountering the healing power of God.

.·◦⊰⊱◦·.

Anna Joy could hardly bend her knees as she packed to attend yet another national conference. The swelling in her legs had increased. She knew her kidneys were failing. "Lord, you know my kidneys are bleeding. I won't be here much longer if you don't do something."

During the service, she sensed the Lord's presence moving over her back. She sensed that God had given her a new kidney. "I'm grateful for the new kidney, Lord, but why didn't you completely heal me?"

"You needed the kidney to live."

.⸙.

At another conference, a healing minister named multiple infirmities the Lord was healing. As the list grew, Anna Joy perched on the edge of her seat. One by one, he ticked off the ailments afflicting her body. *This is me! Is this my time, Lord?*

The speaker concluded this litany of maladies. "And the person being healed is a man."

Anna Joy slumped in her seat and dropped her head into her hands. *Lord, how could you be so cruel?*

"Let's go." Anna Joy mumbled to Debra. She grasped the wheels of her chair, wheeled herself into the restroom, and sobbed. *Lord, I'll need some time to wrestle with you in prayer over this disappointment.*

.⸙.

After traveling to conference after conference, meeting after meeting, the complete healing she longed for still eluded Anna Joy. Twice in the past she'd been told it wasn't time yet. Didn't "not time yet" infer that there was a time for her healing?

She must be doing something wrong. She tried to stop the accusations that circled in her mind—charges from well-meaning people:

"You're not healed because there's sin in your life."

"As a woman in ministry, you are out of God's order."

"You're not submitted under proper headship."

"A woman should not be teaching a man."

She clapped her hands over her ears to silence the cacophony of these naysayers. She had tried to be obedient to Christ, to love the people he had placed along her path.

.⸙.

Over the years, many nationally and internationally known healing ministries had laid hands on her and prayed for Anna Joy's healing.

She appreciated the love and compassion they offered. Even though she still suffered with cerebral palsy after they prayed, she occasionally experienced a strengthening or a brief hiatus from her symptoms.

Anna Joy never gave up praying to the Lord for healing. Over the years as her health deteriorated and she could no longer leave home, she continued to tune in to the television ministries. Their prayers and teachings buoyed her when the waves of discouragement threatened to drown her hope. She also appreciated friends who faithfully prayed and fasted for her. She knew their prayers helped to keep her alive.

"Someday, Lord, I will dance before you completely healed."

55.

The Call of the Bride

My beloved spoke and said to me, "Arise, my
darling, my beautiful one, come with me."

Song of Songs 2:10 (NIV)

"You are my beloved. Will you say yes to being my bride?" Once again, Anna Joy sensed the Lord calling her into a deeper level of intimacy with him. So far, she had avoided giving him an answer.

"I am the Bridegroom you seek," he said. "I am calling you to be consecrated to me and only me."

"I know we are the bride of Christ," Anna Joy said. Maybe she could change the subject. She couldn't even bring herself to read the book of Song of Songs without blushing.

"Lord, you don't necessarily have the best track record with those you called your closest friends," she said. "Peter was crucified, and James was beheaded. Even some of your other saints endured great suffering. Joan of Arc was burned at the stake. Therese of Lisieux died in excruciating pain from tuberculosis. I once heard that Saint

Teresa of Avila, who called you her spouse, said, 'If this is how you treat your friends, no wonder you have so few of them!'"[3]

Would this deeper level of intimacy mean she would experience a greater degree of suffering?

She knew she needed to give the Lord an answer—maybe she would make her decision after the conference she planned to attend in a few weeks. One of the main speakers on the schedule was a nun who was also her friend. She could ask her for spiritual direction.

.ᴓᵉᴓ.

The first night of the conference, one of the speakers stepped up to the microphone and shared a message of encouragement she believed the Lord had placed on her heart for those attending:

> My people, I have called you forth, and you have answered that call. I have beckoned you to come closer, and you have walked softly in my footsteps. I have breathed fire upon you, and you have burned with desire. Your obedience to my calling has touched the hem of my garment. Now I call you into deep waters to bathe your spirit and refresh your soul. As deep calls to deep, so my Father whispers to you, "Come away with me, my beloved." For the breath of the Spirit fills the air. Breathe in. Plunge into the abyss of my love. I call forth my bride. I burn with love for you. You are my prize.

Anna Joy's stomach tightened. *Lord, I didn't come to hear you talk to me about being your bride.*

---

3   Alice Lady Lovat, *The Life of Saint Teresa* (London : Simpkin, Marshall, Hamilton, Kent & Co, 1920) 548, accessed online September 4, 2025, https://archive.org/details/lifeofsaintteres0000unse/page/548/mode/2up.

Anna Joy met with her nun friend. "You know I've never been comfortable with the Lord calling me his beloved and bride, but I think the Lord is asking me to say yes to marrying him. Am I crazy?"

The nun shook her head and smiled. "When Jesus called me to be a nun, I saw a picture of him coming to my house carrying a large box with a big bow. He beamed as he handed me the box. I lifted the lid and pulled out the most beautiful white lace wedding gown. Then he said, 'Will you marry me?' I said, 'Yes!' As I watched him leave, he kicked up his heels, threw his fist in the air, and cried, 'Yes!'

"As nuns, we consecrate ourselves to our divine husband, Christ. It sounds like Jesus is asking you for that level of consecration without the benefit of a convent."

Anna Joy moistened her dry lips. "Sister, I don't know if I can do this."

The nun smiled as she clasped Anna Joy's hands in her own. "You can. Jesus will enable you to do what he is asking of you."

.ᷣᴈᴇᴏ.

Anna Joy found strength and confirmation in the testimony of her friend. When she said yes to the Lord, her turmoil ceased. She began to plan the ceremony for her special day, which she called her Affirmation Day. On this day she would publicly take a vow of chastity and affirm her identity as a bride of Christ. Since green was her favorite color, she would wear a dark green dress. Besides, it would hide any accidents.

But then the Lord reminded her of another word from the conference. "I hold your wedding gown, but your veil will be lifted so I will see your face. I anticipate your coming. The gold ring will not turn to brass. The time is short. There is much to be done. I await your coming, my sister, my bride."

A wedding gown? Did that mean she wouldn't be wearing a green dress? She sensed the Lord say, "My color is not green. My color is red. Do you remember the ruby ring?"

Yes. The ring. Several years earlier, a friend had knocked on her door and said, "The Lord told me to give this ring to you. It's a betrothal ring. It represents the blood of Jesus." Anna Joy had placed the ring on her finger a few times but always returned it to the box and tried to forget about it.

She sensed the Lord wanted her special day to be patterned after a wedding celebration like the ceremony a nun goes through in the convent when she takes her vows.

She remembered her cousin's final vows. Her cousin, Sister Dorothy, had proceeded down the cathedral aisle, along with the other novices, wearing a white wedding gown and veil. They professed their vows of poverty, chastity, and obedience. Just as in a marriage, each received a gold wedding band placed on her left hand. Christ was now their divine husband.

One of Anna Joy's friends volunteered to make her a white wedding dress and veil. "I want my veil made of Alencon lace. It was the lace made by the mother of Saint Therese of Lisieux in Alencon, France. She's my favorite saint."

One day while shopping, Anna Joy spotted a pair of white shoes. "Lord, you know I've never been able to wear white patent leather shoes because of my leg braces. Besides, it's so hard for me to find shoes wide enough for my feet, but I'd like to wear pretty, white shoes for my affirmation."

The clerk knelt in front of her, slipped the shoe on her foot, and buckled the dainty white strap. "How does that feel?"

"We got it on. That's good. Can you stretch it a little?"

"We can try."

When Anna Joy returned to the store, the shoes fit. At least the fit would be tolerable for her special day.

She found a jewelry store that sold Christian jewelry. She selected a gold wedding band with a Hebrew inscription from Ruth 1:16, "Whither thou goest, I will follow."

·◦◦◦·

Preparation for her Affirmation Day included planning the ceremony. She would select the priest, the music, the readings, and share her testimony of how God had prepared her for this special calling.

Anna Joy sat down with one of the priests she knew and shared with him what the Lord had spoken to her.

The priest paged through one of his liturgical books. "We have a special liturgy in the church for those who wish to take a vow of perpetual virginity. I think this is what you are looking for. I can perform this ceremony for you after a Sunday Mass if you would like."

She agreed. But soon after, she discovered the Lord had other ideas regarding her bridal preparation. "I saw a picture of me in a bath filled with red liquid. It was like he was cleansing me with his precious blood. I saw brushes scrubbing me. But these weren't ordinary brushes. Various scriptures were inscribed on each of the bristles. It was like they were washing me with the Word of God just like Scripture says, 'to make her holy and clean, washed by the cleansing of God's word'" (Ephesians 5:26 NLT).

She laughed when she told her friends, "I feel like Queen Esther going through her beauty treatments before marrying the king."

56.

A Heavenly Transport

I know a man in Christ who fourteen years ago was
caught up to the third heaven. Whether it was in the
body or out of the body I do not know—God knows.

2 Corinthians 12:2 (NIV)

Anna Joy prayed between shallow breaths. "Lord, I'm so sick I can hardly breathe, and this pain is unbearable. My legs are cramped and swollen. I don't think I can go on." Scoliosis had twisted her back like a pretzel. She couldn't find a comfortable position to sit or lie. Sleep had eluded her. "I don't know if I'll make it to my Affirmation Day next month."

She had just closed her eyes when she sensed a presence in her room. She blinked, trying to focus on her visitor. "Michael?"

She later shared the sequence of events that followed this visitation. "Michael, the archangel, entered my room. His face glowed. He was huge with golden yellow hair. Even his gown was golden-white. Without a word, he picked me up. He cradled me in his arms like a baby and carried me up through the ceiling, and we floated into the clouds. When I looked down, I saw my body, all twisted, lying on the floor propped up against my pillows. I was so pale.

"It seemed like we shot through the sky until we reached the highest heaven. I was lying limp in his arms and yet aware of my surroundings. Michael carried me across a river that I thought was the River of Life. He carried me along an outdoor path, past children laughing and playing, and into a large, white marbled building. He walked down a long hallway, entered a small room with a marbled table in the center, and laid me on the table. I sensed a presence at my head. I think it was God the Father, but all I saw was his brilliant white hair. I saw Jesus standing on one side of me in a robe of white. On the other side of me, I sensed the Holy Spirit, dazzling and almost translucent. There was another angel nearby, smaller than Michael. I think he was my guardian angel.

"I felt like they had brought me there to give me the will to live. It was as if they were resuscitating me in their presence.

"They dressed me in a finely woven, translucent, red garment. It reminded me of the blood of Jesus. Next they dressed me in my wedding gown, but it wasn't my earthly wedding gown. This wedding gown was made of white lace with my name woven all through the pattern of the lace. They placed a matching veil on my head, bordered with red and white roses. Even my shoes were engraved with my name. I knew they wanted me to go back, but I didn't want to leave. It was so peaceful there, and I had no pain.

"The Lord allowed me to look down toward earth. Again, I saw myself lying on the floor of my bedroom. My friend had brought me Communion and set it down on my cedar chest. I wanted that Communion. So I reached out my hand. Before I knew what was happening, I was back in my body. And back in my room. I'm convinced God had sent that Communion because they knew Communion would draw me back to my earthly body."

Gradually, Anna Joy recovered from her sickness, but the pain remained.

57.

Affirmation Day

For your Maker is your husband, The LORD of hosts is His name.

Isaiah 54:5 (NKJV)

Today was the day. Anna Joy would consecrate herself to the Lord as a bride of Christ. Her insides tingled. Maybe she had wedding jitters like a real bride.

The friend who designed her wedding gown arrived to help her dress. She slipped the white lace gown over Anna Joy's head and buttoned the tiny buttons. Then she buckled Anna Joy's shiny white patent leather shoes. After adjusting the lace mantilla veil, the friend crowned her head with a wreath of red and white roses interwoven with baby's breath.

"You look beautiful. Just like a real bride."

Anna Joy's hands trembled as she fingered her veil, catching one last reflection of herself in the mirror. "I look pretty!"

She carried her new white bridal Bible and a bouquet of red and white roses as she motored into the church in her electric wheelchair.

Her friends flocked around her, offering hugs and encouraging words. She had invited about twenty guests, all special friends she called her spiritual children. They, in turn, called her Mama. But the list didn't include any family members. They wouldn't understand her vow of perpetual virginity as a bride of Christ.

The priest, robed in his vestments, opened the service. "We have come to celebrate the commitment and love you have called your servant, Anna Joy, to step deeper into. You have given your servant the desire to serve you in perpetual chastity. We will now offer the Lord our petitions on her behalf."

After the petitions, the priest invited the community to surround her and pray for her. Many of her friends rose from their seats, laid hands on her, and prayed.

As the church quieted, the priest invited Anna Joy to make her profession of perpetual virginity.

Anna Joy bowed her head. "Lord God, you know the secrets of our hearts. I surrender myself to you. May I strive for excellence in your love. I dedicate myself to you. I dedicate myself to serve those around me. I marvel that you have chosen me to be an instrument. I ask you to bless me now with your abounding love, in the name of the Father, Son, and Holy Spirit."

"We will now have the blessing of the ring." The priest held up the ring with the Hebrew inscription from the book of Ruth, "Whither thou goest, I will follow."

He continued. "The ring is a circle with no beginning or end. As a sign of your love, we bless this ring in the name of the Father, and of the Son, and the Holy Spirit." He handed the ring to the friend Anna Joy had designated to place the ring on her finger. The man knelt on one knee beside her and slipped the ring on her left ring finger.

The priest gave the final blessing. "May your daily life enrich the world and bear fruit. May you live according to the holy virginity you requested. May the Lord fill you with his divine love. May the Lord fill you with a burning desire to serve God's people. Lord, I thank you for her call, commitment, and response. Continue to fill her with your blessings. Amen."

Anna Joy's friend slid onto the piano bench and filled the church with strains of "Joyful, Joyful, We Adore Thee." The children danced and twirled while friends hugged and congratulated Anna Joy.

She returned home to host a smaller celebration with her closest friends. After dropping off their children with babysitters, the guests arrived at her home and received a wedding program. This part of the ceremony reflected her personal testimony of how the Lord had faithfully led her all these years to this day, her Affirmation Day.

The ceremony opened with a time of worship. Then Anna Joy shared her journey. "I knew God was with me even as a child. I lost my mother through divorce because she had to work two jobs and was never home. God knew that a five-year-old needed a mother. That's when Mary, the mother of Jesus, became my friend. She taught me all kinds of things, but she mostly led me straight to Jesus. Sometimes, I also sensed the presence of Michael, the archangel, by my side.

"I also wish to acknowledge and honor some of the people God brought into my life. He gave me a praying grandma. I spent summers with her from the time I was six until I was fifteen. She would wake me up at three in the morning and have me kneel beside her by the bed and pray with her. I couldn't understand anything she prayed because she only prayed in German. At six o'clock, she would tell me I could go back to bed.

"God gave me several other special people who helped me. He gave me an aunt who always believed in me and my cousin Jimmy. He was my protector. God also gave me a friend in my high school teacher Mr. Stevens. He risked his job to mentor me when I was a teenager.

"I was six years old when I received my first call from the Lord. I was preparing for my First Communion with my teacher Sister Mark. I heard the Lord say, 'I want you to be my friend.' That was the first time I heard his voice. I asked Jesus to come into my heart. I said to him, 'I want to belong to you like Sister Mark does. I want to belong to you in spirit, soul, and body.' That was the first time I answered his call to celibacy.

"As a child, I had two dreams. The first was to belong to Jesus. The second dream was that I would have lots of children! I used to sit up at night and think up all kinds of names. I never thought in singles, but twins, triplets, and quadruplets. I think all those names have been used up through all the kids God has given me in the Spirit."

Anna Joy had asked several friends to read the Scriptures the Lord had given her for her Affirmation Day, beginning with Psalm 139.

> For You formed my inward parts;
> You covered me in my mother's womb.
> I will praise You, for I am fearfully and wonderfully made;
> Marvelous are Your works,
> And that my soul knows very well.
> My frame was not hidden from You,
> When I was made in secret,
> And skillfully wrought in the lowest parts of the earth.
> Your eyes saw my substance, being yet unformed.
> And in Your book they all were written,
> The days fashioned for me,
> When as yet there were none of them.
> (Psalm 139:13–16 NKJV)

Next, a friend read from Isaiah 54.

> "Sing, O barren,
> You who have not borne!
> Break forth into singing, and cry aloud,
> You who have not labored with child!
> For more are the children of the desolate
> Than the children of the married woman," says the LORD.'

For your Maker is your husband,
The LORD of hosts is His name;
And your Redeemer is the Holy One of Israel;
He is called the God of the whole earth."
(Isaiah 54:1, 5 NKJV)

"There's a song that has a special significance for me," Anna Joy said. "It's called 'Carpenter Man.' For me, this carpenter man was Jesus. I have two pictures on my wall that remind me of Jesus as a carpenter, one as a child, and the other as a grown man. He was the one who designed the furniture Scott made for me. Scott introduced me to this song and will sing it for us. Just like this song says, he picked me up, twirled me around, and carried me on his shoulders.

"I also have a spiritual mother and father. One night, I planned to commit suicide. The voices in my head were stronger than I was. I prayed. 'If you don't want me to commit suicide, you are going to have to give me the power to resist because these voices are too strong for me.'

"Jesus came through the door and walked into my room. He said, 'I have the power.' He filled me with his Holy Spirit, but I didn't understand what had happened.

"I contacted a priest that I knew, and he said, 'You are either very close to heaven or very close to hell. But I may know someone who can help you.' He introduced me to David, another college student. When he met me, David said, 'I know her.' But I had never met him before. He told me the Lord gave him a vision of me and instructed him to come and pray for me. He became my spiritual father. He also introduced me to Sister Gladys, who became my spiritual mother.

"The Lord brought several other special people into my life. Sister Alphonsus risked her job at the college and her place in the convent to care for me. She demonstrated pure, unadulterated love." Anna Joy went on to say that her ministry was a combination of the ministries of Sister Alphonsus and Sister Gladys. "The Lord gave me two special friends in Gert and Ruby. Both are intercessors, and because of their prayers, I'm alive today.

"When I received a second call to belong to Jesus, I thought he meant I should join a convent. I wrote letters to every convent in the country, but I received no response, so I dropped it. I guess they didn't want someone who was disabled. I even bought a ring, but I lost it."

Anna Joy paused while another friend read from Psalm 45.

Listen, O daughter,
Consider and incline your ear;
Forget your own people also, and your father's house;
So the King will greatly desire your beauty;
Because He is your Lord, worship Him.
(Psalm 45:10–11 NKJV)

Anna Joy also chose the following Scriptures from John 15 and Revelation 4.

"You are My friends if you do whatever I command you. No longer do I call you servants, for a servant does not know what his master is doing; but I have called you friends, for all things that I heard from My Father I have made known to you. You did not choose Me, but I chose you and appointed you that you should go and bear fruit, and that your fruit should remain, that whatever you ask the Father in My name He may give you." (John 15:14–16 NKJV)

"Thou art worthy, O Lord, to receive glory and honour and power: for thou hast created all things, and for thy pleasure they are and were created." (Revelation 4:11 KJV)

Anna Joy continued. "One time, when I was on stage with my traveling singing group, I sensed the Lord saying to me, 'You were created for my pleasure.'

"I heard the third call four years ago. I was at a conference when they called for those with religious vocations to come up to the platform. Since I felt I had no calling to a religious vocation, I just sat there minding my own business. Then I heard an audible voice from the Lord. 'You should be up there.' I just closed my eyes. I wasn't going up to the front. I felt three hands on my shoulders. *Who laid hands on me?* I sensed the Lord say, 'There are three of us, and we all laid hands on you. I'm calling you again. We need celibate people.'

"I went home and prayed. I sensed the Lord saying, 'I meant it when I called you. Why didn't you answer? You were supposed to respond to me, not write letters to convents.'

"At the conference this past summer, one of the words spoken from the platform seemed like it was just for me. 'I hold your wedding gown, but your veil will be lifted so I will see your face. I anticipate your coming. The gold ring will not turn to brass. The time is short, and there is much to be done. I await your coming, my sister, my bride.' I remembered the ruby betrothal ring the Lord had given me several years before, which I had tried to forget.

"The Lord told me, 'You are in good company. Like Moses, you've had forty years between your first call and your answer.'"

Another friend stepped forward and read the Scriptures Anna Joy had chosen.

> For I wish that all men were even as I myself. But each one has his own gift from God, one in this manner and another in that. But I say to the unmarried and to the widows: It is good for them if they remain even as I am. (1 Corinthians 7:7–8 NKJV)

Another friend read the next Scripture about the alabaster jar.

> Then Mary took a pound of very costly oil of
> spikenard, anointed the feet of Jesus, and wiped His
> feet with her hair. And the house was filled with the
> fragrance of the oil. (John 12:3 NKJV)

"Some may think I'm being wasted, but I'm not wasted, I'm poured out for you.

"The Lord gave me one last confirmation at the conference. Jesus handed me his heart. My heart grew and became part of his heart. Then he said, 'You are bone of my bone and flesh of my flesh. You are mine.'

"One day I watched as my spiritual mother, Sister Gladys, prayed over all the people at a healing service. I sensed God saying to me, 'I am going to pass her ministry to you.' I said no. 'Let me show you what it will cost you,' he said. He showed me her heart broken five million times over. I wasn't very happy about this. That's when I heard the song, 'Here I Am Lord' before it was even written. As we sing this song, I open my hands to the Lord and say, 'Here I am, Lord, send me.'"

After the song, Anna Joy declared her response to the Lord's call on her life. "Lord, you have said I am your song. Lord, you have said I am your joy. Lord, you have said I am a gift to you, the Father, the Son, and the Holy Spirit. Lord, you have said I'm a gift to your people. I can say with you, I am altogether beautiful, and there is no blemish in me. I agree with your estimation of me when you say who I am. I say, 'Yes, Lord.'"

Anna Joy's guests responded with the song, "God Danced the Day You Were Born," followed by an invitation to lay hands on her and pray as the Lord would lead.

One after another shared words of blessing over her.

One of the women prayed, "Holy Spirit, give me words for Anna Joy. Thank you, Lord." She continued, "My child, my sister, my bride, I thank you. I've waited many long years for you to come to me. For you to hold your head up proud and say of Jesus, 'He is my Bridegroom.' My child, my sister, my bride, I have loved you so long, I have waited so long for your joyous return."

Another friend spoke, "I hear the Lord saying, 'I sing to you, my darling. I sing to you, my love. Do not be afraid. Come meet your Bridegroom. Don't be afraid. I welcome you. I welcome you with songs of joy, my gift, my bride, my love, my spouse.'"

Another friend shared a word. "I can see heaven. There are no crutches, no handicap, no glasses. Jesus declares to all the heavenly hosts, 'This is my bride. This is my beloved. This is my chosen.'"

After words from the Lord and prayers were shared, the time had come for a final blessing. "May the Lord bless you and keep you. May the Lord's face shine upon you and be gracious to you and give you peace."

Anna Joy scanned the beaming faces of her friends, faces that reflected the joy bubbling inside of her. "I want to thank you all for sharing this special day with me. Now, what would a wedding be without a wedding cake?"

Anna Joy had selected a chocolate sheet cake with vanilla icing. Green leaves intertwined with the red and white roses bordering the inscription: *Anna Joy, Song of Joy, Gift of God.*

58.

Triumphant Through Christ

Now thanks be to God who always leads us in
triumph in Christ, and through us diffuses the
fragrance of His knowledge in every place.

2 Corinthians 2:14 (NKJV)

After the affirmation, Anna Joy knew that her relationship with the Lord had changed. Her intimacy with Jesus had deepened, and as a believer, she became increasingly aware of her authority in Christ.

One day while in prayer, she sensed the Lord transporting her in the Spirit to the second heaven. He paraded her in front of the demonic hosts and announced, "This is my bride. She has authority over you, and you will obey her."

Anna Joy shrank back. "No, Lord! Don't say that! I don't want to be a target for them any more than I already am."

"No, they know you have authority over them. I want them to know that *you* know you have authority over them."

.⸱⸱⸱.

Her authority in Christ was put to the test one morning when she awoke with pain piercing her right eye. Her eye felt swollen shut, as though it was being pushed out of its socket. Anna Joy saw a picture of a tumor covering the whole right side of her head and face. She rebuked the tumor in Jesus's name. She then heard the words, "Take Communion." She immediately took Communion.

In the Spirit, she heard the demons growl. "You need to quit what you're doing, and we'll leave you alone." She sensed they intended to possess the right side of her body.

"I won't quit, and I can't give you my body."

They howled. As they slunk away, she heard them grumble, "Lucifer should do his own dirty work."

She had refused to give them permission to possess her body because her body belonged to the Lord, and she had his body. This concept was a major revelation for her and a new weapon in her arsenal against the Enemy. She sensed the Enemy tried to cause her to have a stroke. But God intervened and healed her.

.ᴄᴏᴌᴇᴐ.

During this season, she wrote a letter to a friend:

> Just a few lines, and more than a few moments to tell you
> that my thoughts and even plans have been focused on
> you and several others to write to for the last few weeks.
> The envelopes are stamped and addressed and lying
> beside my pillow. I just have to wait on my hands and the
> ability to write. Then your letter and call came. Sorry I
> couldn't talk.
>
> My counseling and praying goes on whether sick or well.
> I'm always happy to hear from you. I have been very sick,
> but I am recovering now. I don't get out a lot because of
> growing weakness, but God is faithful to stay with me,
> giving me his wonderful presence, and a knowledge of
> himself and his love for us that is comforting. He has

again said I shall live and not die and see the goodness of the Lord in the land of the living.

He has been showing me the benefits of his death, and I am becoming part of it. It frees me from the law, sin, my past, and fear of the unknown, to rise to live by his grace, blood, life, Spirit, and power. I am just learning, but I am indeed crucified with Jesus and buried with him in water baptism. Applying it is a constant job, but certainly gives me a starting point that's victorious, giving me leverage over the Enemy if I'll use it. The broken bread is one way of partaking of Jesus's death, his brokenness that bought our wholeness. The blood is his life. The key to living for him is recognizing I died with him when I was born again—the sinful me, and buried that part of me in water baptism, and/or the blood. It was already done, but I have to apply it daily. But I can make a choice to let Jesus live his life through me through the power of his Spirit. Does it hurt? Yes. Is it easy? No. Fast? No. But it is a fact. I can choose to let Jesus make it real.

The Litany of Humility is what I have to die to. Hard but possible because God gives me his character, life, etc. So freeing. I am dependent on God to live my new (his) life through me. I am reluctant to do what is right (rebellious). I have a right to my life, my feelings, even though it makes me miserable. He will never let me do destructive things if I trust him and live his way. I don't have to protect myself from abuse. He will do that by causing me to stand against evil. That is what I have been learning. How God loves me and desires my company. How my life is Jesus himself— his life. Now I realize this by giving up, dying to my own life, by my choice and his grace, power, and Spirit. I am excited, hopeful, and growing again.

Regarding a concert Anna Joy attended by a contemporary Christian artist, she wrote,

> He was so good. He did a section of songs about the value of handicapped lives. It was good for me. He also majored on how God adores us and desires to be with us.
>
> I have enclosed the Litany of Humility for you.

Litany of Humility

O Jesus, meek and humble of heart,
Hear me.

From the desire of being esteemed,
Deliver me, O Jesus.

From the desire of being loved,
Deliver me, O Jesus.

From the desire of being extolled,
Deliver me, O Jesus.

From the desire of being honored,
Deliver me, O Jesus.

From the desire of being praised,
Deliver me, O Jesus.

From the desire of being preferred to others,
Deliver me, O Jesus.

From the desire of being consulted,
Deliver me, O Jesus.

From the desire of being approved,
Deliver me, O Jesus.

From the fear of being humiliated,
Deliver me, O Jesus.

From the fear of being despised,
Deliver me, O Jesus.

From the fear of suffering rebukes,
Deliver me, O Jesus.

From the fear of being calumniated,
Deliver me, O Jesus.

From the fear of being forgotten,
Deliver me, O Jesus.

From the fear of being ridiculed,
Deliver me, O Jesus.

From the fear of being wronged,
Deliver me, O Jesus.

From the fear of being suspected,
Deliver me, O Jesus.

That others may be loved more than I,
Jesus, grant me the grace to desire it.

That others may be esteemed more than I,
Jesus, grant me the grace to desire it.

That, in the opinion of the world, others
may increase, and I may decrease,
Jesus, grant me the grace to desire it.

That others may be chosen and I set aside,
Jesus, grant me the grace to desire it.

That others may be praised and I go unnoticed,
Jesus, grant me the grace to desire it.

That others may be preferred to me in everything,
Jesus, grant me the grace to desire it.

That others may become holier than I, provided that I may become
as holy as I should,
Jesus, grant me the grace to desire it.[4]

---

4   Attributed to Cardinal Rafael Merry del Val (1865–1930), however, the author is considered unknown, and versions were written before his. It is a public domain prayer. The version above appears here: https://www.ewtn.com/catholicism/devotions/litany-of-humility-245.

59.

Cloistered

*But when you pray, go away by yourself, shut the door
behind you, and pray to your Father in private.*

Matthew 6:6 (NLT)

Anna Joy plopped to the floor and sobbed. "Lord, I can't do it! I can't pull myself up into the wheelchair." Sweat dripped down her face, mingling with her tears. She had spent the better part of an hour gripping the armrests of her wheelchair and trying to hoist her bottom off the floor without success. No matter how she positioned her legs, her muscles refused to cooperate. She couldn't muster the strength to lift her body off the floor. *Lord, if I can't get up, I'm afraid I'll never be able to leave my home again.*

Once again, her body betrayed her, just as it had done several years earlier when she lacked the strength to walk with her crutches. At that time, she had resigned herself to a wheelchair for mobility.

A friend visiting from out of town offered her some insight. "I believe the Lord is answering the prayer you prayed many years ago. You asked him for a cloistered community. He has given you the cloister you prayed for. Now you can spend more time with the Lord in prayer."

.∽⊱⊰∽.

Anna Joy wrote in a letter to a friend:

> I wanted to share the definition of silence I found in
> Scripture in the Amplified Bible that has really blessed me.
> Psalm 65:1 says, "To You belongs silence (the submissive
> wonder of reverence, which bursts forth into praise) and
> praise is due and fitting to You, O God, in Zion; and to You
> shall the vow be performed."[5]
>
> God has been giving me lots of music and praise. He
> certainly is very worthy of it. He is a great and mighty
> God, a wonderful Lord and Father.

.⋄◦⋄.

For the next seven years, Anna Joy was unable to leave her home.
Eventually her body weakened to the point she could no longer
leave her bedroom—a bedroom bisected by a bed she could no
longer sleep in. A bed monopolized by her stuffed cats. She slept on
a plastic mat, her pain-wracked body supported by a pile of green
pillows. A stack of Bibles remained within arm's reach. Pictures of
friends, family, and Siamese cats lined her walls along with pictures of Jesus portrayed as the carpenter, the lion, and the Good
Shepherd.

As her physical world grew smaller, her scope of prayer widened,
more far-reaching than she could have imagined. She frequently
prayed between the hours of three and six in the morning. Her grandmother had prepared her well for this call since she had awakened
Anna Joy as a child to pray in the wee hours of the morning. The
Lord impressed this thought upon her spirit: *You are one of a select
group of continental intercessors. Your assignment is North America.*

---

5   Amplified® Bible (AMPC), Copyright © 1954, 1958, 1962, 1964, 1965, 1987 by
The Lockman Foundation. Used by permission. lockman.org

.ᴼᴼᴼᴼᴼ.

During prayer one night, Anna Joy sensed she had somehow been transported to the hospital room of a friend's father. He seemed agitated, clawing through his bedclothes as if looking for something. *Did he need his call light?* Anna Joy sat with him and prayed until he calmed down and fell asleep.

On another occasion, a friend's mother lay dying in the hospital. Anna Joy found herself sitting by the woman's bedside, holding her hand. After the woman's death, the Lord gave Anna Joy a picture of the woman and her husband in heaven. She was a great lady in heaven and tended his gardens. A perfect heavenly assignment for this earthly florist. She also saw a picture of the woman's husband in heaven. He wore coveralls and cared for the Lord's white horses.

Several times, Anna Joy found herself, in a way that seems unexplainable, transported in the Spirit by helicopter on rescue missions in war-torn countries. She discovered that God could transcend time and physical boundaries just like he did with Philip. (See Acts 8:38–40.)

After 9/11, she sensed the Lord had assigned her a birthing intercession for triplets. *Who are these babies, Lord?*

"You are carrying an intercession for revival. One of the babies represents revival in the United States, one is for revival in Israel, and the third is for a revival among the Muslim nations."

Anna Joy's intercessions required increasingly intense prayer. One day she sensed an evil presence enter her bedroom. She couldn't catch her breath. The presence seemed to suck the air out of the room. In their verbal exchange, she repeatedly responded, "I will not! I will not stop praying for the Muslim nations."

The evil presence left, but not before he snarled departing threats. "Your prayers will cost you your life. You don't want to die, do you?"

"I will do anything for Jesus," she said.

Oxygen seemed to rush back into the room. Anna Joy drew in a deep breath—fresh air.

.⁊ℓ⁊.

Later the Lord asked her, "Are you willing to pray to the death? I have so few intercessors who are willing to pray if it will cost them their life. Will you pray?"

If I say yes, am I going to die?

She sensed the Lord tell her that yes, she may die because of the intercessory appointments. "Will you pray anyway?"

"Yes, I'll pray." She would pray even if it cost her life. She would do whatever the Lord asked of her.

.⁊ℓ⁊.

One day she felt the birthing process in prayer completed for the revivals in the United States and Israel. But she sensed the Muslim revival was not progressing as it should. As an intercessor, she knew that sometimes she needed the help of another prayer warrior when an intercession felt stuck.

A friend of hers arrived in town specifically to help her pray through the Muslim revival intercession. For several hours, they groaned in prayer and prayed. But when this intercession was finally birthed, this baby was not a baby, but a small child. No wonder he was stuck. This revival needed to be born running to survive. After the completion of this intercession, Anna Joy heard stories about Muslims in various countries in which Jesus appeared to them in dreams. Many believed in Jesus as Savior and Lord.

60.

Letters to a Friend

So encourage each other and build each other
up, just as you are already doing.

1 Thessalonians 5:11 (NLT)

Anna Joy treasured her correspondence, even more so since her physical condition had confined her to a very limited space on the floor of her bedroom, propped up on pillows. Letters, phone calls, and visits were her only personal contact with the outside world.

Anna Joy wrote to her friend Kelly:

> You have been on my mind and heart for some time. I miss you. I'd really like to see you or talk to you, but I never know when you are free, since you are committed on so many fronts. So, I thought a letter would be the least intrusive way to talk to you since I don't have a computer. I don't want one—too weak. It's labor-intensive for me. Besides, a letter, call, or visit is more personal. You deserve my time and efforts. Unfortunately, that delays the writing until I am able and alone. I am a slow writer. This is stamped but not yet written.

I wanted to tell you how much I appreciate God's blessing through the notes, the visits, your support, care, and, I'm sure, prayers. The $700 in August was part of an answer to a very specific personal prayer. I ask God to return the blessing many times over. You know the joy of God, proof he hears you, I am sure. He also made my birthday and that month special. It's usually an emotional and financial downer. That too was part of my August prayer. God is truly great and good! I try to fill my calendar with reasons to rejoice. Sometimes I need to remember my blessings, of which people are the greatest. He only gives me the best. That includes you.

It's truly fall here—colorful trees and flowers—crisp, but usually sunny days. Cold nights, at least cool. We've had frosts. Our growing season is over, but harvest is here. Concord grapes, my favorites for eating, and crisp, crunchy apples and pickles. It's beautiful. So many proofs of God's generous provision and presence. A celebration of overflowing life. It makes me feel alive and able. Not at all fifty-five and a senior citizen. The year, season, and my life are in the same place—the best time. Of course, all times are the best since we walk in and with God. I hope I've gained God's benefit to seniors—wisdom. I am truly grateful for each year and their gifts to me. I like the times God has given me, if not always the circumstances.

I am in the midst of an ongoing and serious intercession for the USA and revival worldwide. So many don't know Jesus. He misses them. So, I am praying for the relief of his pain, which can only happen through the salvation of souls. Please add prayers for all intercessors to the others you pray for if he leads.

I'd be interested in hearing about you if you are inclined.

God loves, hears, and walks with you. May you live in his manifest presence. I am praying for you and love you.

.ༀ.

The next year, Anna Joy wrote another letter to Kelly. She had selected a notecard from her rubber-banded stack: a small child playing in the sand. Perfect for the beginning of summer. She recalled how she loved digging her toes into the wet sand, the way the granules cooled and tickled her feet. She sighed. Those days were over.

A clap of thunder interrupted her musings. Her eyes shot toward the window as lightning flashed. She shuddered. She hated being alone during a storm, and Debra had left for work. She remembered being alone as a child when a tornado whipped through their trailer park. The trailer rattled and shook as the winds blew and rain pelted the metal roof. Thankfully neither she nor her brother had been injured. He had thrown himself into a ditch just as the tornado rotated above him. The memory of that too-close-for-comfort storm still traumatized her.

With a shaky hand, she picked up her pen. Time to focus on her letter. Maybe writing the letter would provide a distraction.

Jesus is Lord!

This card reminds me of how we are in God's sight—a child. A state we need to recognize in order to enter the kingdom of God, and then to be able to see where we are. We are totally dependent on God, who has given us the faith we need to know he can and will help us. I'm more and more aware of how much I need him, without or with my health or handicap. I hope I always remember how he has helped when my situation changes. I also hope I remember I'll still need him just as much for everything. God is good, faithful, and unchanging.

Memorial Day weekend, I began to remember the people
who died so I could be free and/or live. Foremost and
first would be Jesus—praise his name and faithfulness.
God spoke to me to remember, bless, and thank him,
and them, the living people who are doing the same for
me today. Then all the people he has shared with me, his
treasures and mine. Like you. I've thanked God for you,
for his willingness to share with me a very unique, special,
valuable treasure like YOU! Thanks for your friendship,
faithfulness, prayers, visits, support, and money. I pray
your reward will be a hundredfold, for you have given
much more than a cup of water. I know you won't lose your
reward since he promised that—just that some of them will
be in this life. May his presence always go with you.

It's 2:00 a.m. and storming. Debra's working, and I can't
sleep, so I'm slowly writing this letter.

My situation continues: I continue to lose weight, except
for my stomach, suffer pain at times, the disabling kind,
and bleeding. Prayer does make a definite difference in
duration of sieges of pain, intensity, and ability to bear
it. Eating, sleeping, and going to the bathroom remain
problems, but God is faithful, even to tasty recipes I would
like and can eat. Prayer helps. Appreciate it.

I'm praying for you—Love you—thanks again—Big hugs.

Anna Joy wrote to Kelly again the following summer:

You have been on my mind and heart and in my prayers.
How has your summer gone? Some of the services you
mentioned being a part of sound really neat! I would like
to do something like that. But each of us must do what

God gives us to do. For me that's mostly prayer. My prayer for you is that God will restore the joy of his salvation in you. I want to present two things to you to consider. Your joy has not gone away, only your experience of it. Very important, I admit. Joy is rooted in the presence of God. He's still within you and with you in the person of the Holy Spirit. His presence, power, and joy enable us to keep going. For which I thank him since we would surely fail without his strength.

Second, God is concerned with faithfulness, which is tested in hard times and places, when feeling is gone or opposing us, and his manifest presence is absent. It didn't help me to know I walked by faith, because faith was intangible, and not always easily accessed, until I realized I believed, loved, served, obeyed, and trusted a person. A person I could know by studying Jesus—his express image. His life was written down. So I could read it, know him, and imitate him.

Believing what is written is a choice I make every day, whether or not my circumstances agree with it. I BELIEVE God is who he said he is and who Jesus demonstrated him to be. I BELIEVE he keeps his Word, and he is able to perform it. And he will. My job is to choose, his to enable. I trust he will. For all of us.

You are God's reflection and blessing. I am praying for you. I love you. Come see us when you can.

Kelly arrived for Anna Joy's birthday the following month. Anna Joy was too ill to enjoy her special birthday dinner, but she was grateful her friend had come to spend time with her. Little did they know, it would be their last time together.

61.

The Cross

Yet indeed I also count all things loss for the excellence of the
knowledge of Christ Jesus my Lord, for whom I have suffered the
loss of all things, and count them as rubbish, that I may gain Christ.

Philippians 3:8 (NKJV)

Once again, Anna Joy couldn't sleep. She gasped for air despite the multiple fans set on high, blasting cool air at her sweat-streaked face. Anna Joy sensed the Holy Spirit whisper, *Breathe, breathe.* On the nights she struggled to breathe, she called him her Holy Ghost breathing machine. She fought for life with every ounce of strength because God had commanded, *Choose life.* She obeyed, even when her body begged to surrender.

During the blackness of night, she often faced the darkest opposition from the Enemy. One night while alone, she had an accident involving diarrhea. She took off her clothes and tried to clean herself as well as the floor. Suddenly, she fell face down in the pool of diarrhea. She sobbed. "The Enemy has won!"

The Lord spoke to her. "The Enemy only wins if you don't get back up. It's in the getting back up that you win."

Anna Joy lifted her head, pulled herself up, and slammed her fist on the floor. Through gritted teeth, she spat, "I win!"

.❦.

Anna Joy loved the cross and often meditated on the crucifixion, more so as her own suffering increased. One day she asked Jesus to take her to the cross. He granted her request and allowed her to see his bruised and bloody body hanging on the cross at Calvary. So repulsed by how marred and disfigured he appeared, she averted her gaze. Jesus talked to her about turning away. He asked her, "Can you still love me?" Yes, she still loved Jesus. He was all she had, and she clung to him.

As her pain and suffering increased, she sensed the Lord draw her deeper into his Passion. She had experienced the sting of betrayal, the loss of relationships, and the depletion of her finances as loved ones dropped their financial support. Pain stabbed her body. Her blankets became like heavy weights over her body, increasing her pain. At night, she tossed aside these weighty covers and lay on the cold floor, wet and shivering.

Anna Joy loved to hug people and receive hugs. One of the hardest crosses to bear was the pain that resulted from hugging. She'd steel herself for each approaching hug, anticipating the fiery pain that would shoot throughout her nerve endings.

"Lord, I wish I could take pain meds. But I can't go to a doctor. They'll demand more procedures. I can't do that again." She struggled to take another breath. "Besides, I don't tolerate any pain medications. I know they make me sick. I can't even take anti-inflammatories because they stop my kidneys, and I swell up like a balloon."

She knew a hospital was not an option. She recalled the Lord telling her that if she went back to a hospital, she would never come home.

Sometimes when the pain was at its worst, Jesus, in his mercy, carried her into his secret place. In this place, the love and peace of Jesus enveloped her, overrode the pain, and released her temporarily from suffering.

62.

Free at Last

We would rather be away from these earthly bodies,
for then we will be at home with the Lord.

2 Corinthians 5:8 (NLT)

One month after Kelly's visit, the Lord directed Catherine to clear her calendar and visit Anna Joy. A new sickness had racked Anna Joy's body, assaulted her lungs, and further compromised her breathing.

Anna Joy's eyes searched her friend's face. "Am I going to die?"

"I don't know. When I came in the spring, it was because the Lord told me you were dying, and he wanted you to live." She paused for a moment. "I'm sorry. This time he is silent."

Anna Joy slumped back into her pillows and closed her eyes. "He didn't warn me."

.ᴐᴑᴇᴐ.

One evening, Anna Joy's pale face beamed as she pulled herself up from her stack of pillows. "The Lord gave me a vision. In it, both good and bad angels were preparing celebrations in the heavenlies on the same level. It's something big. I'm to come. They have my wedding dress ready for me to wear, but the dress is fuller. The same veil, but a different crown. The crown of a wife, and not the crown of a bride. Michael will come to keep me safe. In my vision, all the warring angels were in military garb. Jesus was dressed like a king, just like when we got married. There was no talking in heaven in this vision, just gestures, and all the angels were doing whatever they were supposed to be doing.

"This will be a celebration for the intercessors, and they all get to go. Both good and evil angels are preparing for a celebration of victory. The Enemy's preparations are very noisy.

"Michael brought the wedding dress and said that when it's time, someone will come and help me dress. Michael will be dressed in battle uniform. He told me that I was doing just fine. He said the Lord is calling some of his continental intercessors to come home."

.ᴏᴏɭᴇᴏ.

Anna Joy's body continued to weaken. She slept, rarely speaking. She had plugged *The Hiding Place* into her DVD player and pressed continuous play. She especially related to Betsy since Betsy struggled with her health. Eventually, Betsy succumbed to her sickness and died during her internment as a political prisoner in a Nazi concentration camp.

Anna Joy had been minimally responsive when a friend came to sit with her. She opened her glassy eyes and mumbled. "Get my dress."

"Which dress?" The friend went to the closet and pulled out a red dress. "This dress?"

"No, not that one." Anna Joy dismissed her friend with a frail wave of her hand. "Never mind," she muttered in a disgusted tone and closed her eyes.

Later that day, Anna Joy's friends gathered around her and prayed. She struggled to breathe, each gasp shallow and strained. A friend gently held Anna Joy up to help her breathe, supporting the weight of her body as she fought for air. But as the pain intensified, her friend laid her back down again against her wall of pillows.

Suddenly, Anna Joy grinned and raised herself off her pillows. Her previously dull eyes sparkled as she flapped her arms and squealed, "I'm free! I'm free!" As quickly as she rose, she fell back onto her pillows and closed her eyes.

Several hours later, she was free from all earthly suffering.

.ᨆᨆ.

Anna Joy was laid to rest clothed in her earthly wedding dress. A wreath of red and white roses encircled her veil. God is faithful. He had called his bride home.

> For our present troubles are small and won't last
> very long. Yet they produce for us a glory that vastly
> outweighs them and will last forever!
>
> 2 Corinthians 4:17 (NLT)

63.

Epilogue

Remembrance of Anna Joy

by Pastor Tess Brunmeier

I have the honor today to say a few words about Anna Joy. I know we have mixed emotions today, symbolized by this dress I'm wearing. Notice the black and gold stripes on my dress. The black symbolizes the grief we feel, our sadness, and the loss of our close friend, sister, daughter, cousin, niece, leader, and mama. [6]

The gold symbolizes the reality that Anna Joy is now in heaven with her Lord and Savior, Jesus Christ. She is finally free to run, jump, and dance as a bride of Christ. She is HIS Song of Joy, his gift. We are both sad and yet full of hope, knowing Anna Joy is now receiving her reward in heaven.

Anna Joy was the holiest person I've ever known. Even in death, she looks like a saint. She was a mentor and spiritual mama to many whom she affectionately referred to as "her kids." She would tirelessly listen to us as we cried on the phone or in her room. She would counsel us, love us unconditionally, and pray for us.

---

6   Reproduced by permission from Pastor Tess Brunmeier, 2003.

Anna Joy knew how to pray. She wouldn't just pray for a specific request or problem, but also for our families, coworkers, friends, and people in our lives. She was an intercessor, one who prayed intensely, on a level we only read about from the saints of the past. She gave every breath, every pain, and even her very life in her role as a prayer warrior. She had a view into the spiritual world that exists around us, one that most people are not willing to pay the price to enter. It was God who directed her prayers, and she knew God's voice. He called her to pray for cities, states, countries, and nations. She surrendered her will and her life to obey God's call to live and intercede.

But in all of this, she was often misunderstood. In the midst of her physical pain and suffering, she was filled with joy. She was God's Song of Joy. Her relationship with the Father, Son, and Holy Spirit was so intimate that she was consumed by God's love and freely shared that love with us. She persevered, not giving in to self-pity or depression, but choosing LIFE. In joy, she gave and gave and gave.

As we pause to reflect on the times we've spent with Anna Joy, we remember her love of life, her childlike sense of wonder at God's creativity and goodness, her smile, her singing with abandon to the Lord, her laughter, her contagious joy, her love of flowers and pretty things like jewelry, crystals that reflected rainbows, and cuddly animals like lions, cats, and especially Siamese kittens!

When I was preparing this, I wondered, "What would Anna Joy want me to say to everyone gathered here?" I think she would want me to say:

"Love Jesus! Serve the Lord with all your heart, mind, soul, and strength! Become devoted to God. Seek after Jesus. If you don't know him, seek him and he will find you. Make your life count for the kingdom of God.

"Turn your grief into action—pray, visit shut-ins, those in nursing homes, the elderly, and the sick. Speak up and protect the weak and the poor. Look for those who are overlooked in this world and love them."

Our lives have been changed because we knew Anna Joy. In the midst of our grief, our hope is sparked. We know we will see her again in heaven. Everyone in this room benefited from her prayers, whether you knew it or not. Let her life continue to influence us as we go forward from this day to love God and love each other just like Anna Joy did for us.

Jesus, please tell Anna Joy for us: We love you, we miss you, and we will see you again soon.

Afterword

A Reflection After Anna Joy's Passing

For now we see only a reflection as in a mirror; then
we shall see face to face. Now I know in part; then
I shall know fully, even as I am fully known.

1 Corinthians 13:12 (NIV)

About a year after Anna Joy's passing, I attended a Christian event held in a large arena. It had been a long, painful season—one marked by questions and grief as I struggled to hold on to hope.

As I stood in that arena surrounded by thousands of believers, my voice joined theirs in worshipping Jesus. Choruses of voices singing, "All hail the power of Jesus' name," and then, "Crown him with many crowns, the Lamb upon the throne," reverberated throughout the rafters. Suddenly I sensed something shift in the atmosphere as we sang these familiar hymns. They were fuller, weightier, as if we were joined by a heavenly choir.

And then it happened.

I heard a familiar voice—clear, joyful, unmistakably hers—rising above the sound of the crowd: "It's true! It's true! It's all true!"

My heart leaped. *Anna Joy?* How could this be? I scanned the crowd. But she wasn't there.

287

I can't logically explain what I heard, but in my spirit, I knew. Even though she wasn't physically present in the arena, she was very much alive—alive in the presence of her Savior. She didn't just believe the words we sang in those hymns anymore. She lived in the fullness of the truth those old hymns proclaimed.

The lyrics that filled the arena weren't just songs we sing in church. These hymns reflected the eternal glory of God—the glory Anna Joy now sees with her own eyes before the throne of Christ, surrounded by the worship of saints and angels.

So now, when I sing those old hymns—when I hear the words of "Crown Him with Many Crowns" or "All Hail the Power of Jesus' Name," I remember that moment. I remember her voice.

And I remember the joy that came with knowing:

It's true. It's all true.

Joanie

Acknowledgments

My deep appreciation and gratitude to all those who have made this book possible. Thank you to everyone who shared their correspondence and their memories with me—your contributions have brought greater meaning and depth to her story.

Mom (Luella Shawhan). You opened the door to the world of books for me. Every time the school flyer came home, you never hesitated—you always purchased the stack I requested. Because of you, reading became a lifelong gift.

Pastor Tess Brunmeier. I am deeply grateful for your generosity in allowing me to share your beautiful words. I so appreciate your friendship. Being able to share your moving eulogy was both an honor and a comfort. Thank you.

Rabbi Glenn David Blank. Thank you for your friendship and support. Your uplifting foreword brings hope to those in need of encouragement.

Intercessory Prayer Team. Anna Joy's story could not have been told without the power of intercessory prayer. I want to thank the faithful prayer warriors who continually lifted me up as I wrote. Your love, prayers, and unwavering support through the years mean more to me than words can express.

Friends of the Pen. I have learned so much from each of you as we've shared our writing journeys together. Anita Klumpers, Lori Lipsky, and Robin Steinweg—your guidance, encouragement, and friendship have shaped me into a better writer. I'm grateful for every word, every critique, and every moment we've spent growing together.

Kathy Carlton Willis. I honestly can't thank you enough for all the mentoring, teaching, encouragement, brainstorming, networking, and wisdom you've poured into me. You've shown up with generosity and heart time and time again, and it's made such a difference in my life. I've grown so much because of your influence, and I'm incredibly grateful—not just for what you've taught me, but for who you are.

WordGirls. I am grateful for each of you in this amazing writing community mentored by Kathy Carlton Willis. Through our shared journey, we have not only developed our craft as writers but have also grown in faith—encouraging one another and lifting each other up in prayer.

Michelle Rayburn. Thank you so much for your meticulous attention to detail in editing and typesetting my manuscript, as well as for the beautiful cover design. Your expertise and care have made a meaningful difference, and I'm truly grateful for your dedication in bringing my work to life.

To Our Lord Jesus Christ, I am deeply grateful for your divine hand in bringing this spiritual mama into my life. You knew exactly what I needed to grow in faith and understanding. I dedicate this work to your glory.

About the Author

Joanie Shawhan shares true-life stories, offering her readers an eye-witness view of the action. Her Selah Awards Finalist book *In Her Shoes: Dancing in the Shadow of Cancer* reflects the value of "Your story plus my story become our stories." An ovarian cancer survivor and registered nurse, Joanie speaks to medical students in the Survivors Teaching Students program. She co-founded an ovarian cancer social group: The Fried Eggs—Sunny-Side Up. She has contributed to multiple anthologies and devotionals. Follow Joanie at www.joanieshawhan.com.

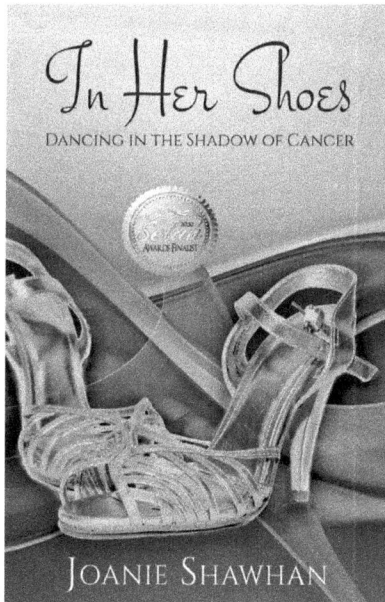

"Joanie Shawhan has captured the life of her wise mentor and friend in this book. She has handed us a descriptive photo album of a life full of trials, yet we see Anna Joy allowing God to lead through each one. God is near in both joy and suffering. The woman pictured was a spiritual mentor for me and for hundreds of people. Her true-life stories give us courage to follow Jesus no matter what happens in our lives."

—PASTOR TESS GITTER BRUNMEIER (Vineyard Church USA) BS education, MA psychological counseling, MDiv, and PhD (ABD) church history

www.ingramcontent.com/pod-product-compliance
Lightning Source LLC
Chambersburg PA
CBHW062044080426
42734CB00012B/2557